THE SALMON AND SEA TROUT RIVERS OF ENGLAND AND WALES (V. 1)

D1664178

THE SALMON AND SEA TROUT RIVERS OF ENGLAND AND WALES (V. 1)

Augustus Grimble

A General Books LLC Publication.

CONTENTS

1

SECTION 1

The Salmon and Sea Trout Rivers of England and Wales
Chapter I

THE TEST

T S typical more or less of the other chalk streams of the South of England which hold salmon, for they all flow at a fairly rapid pace under plenty of bridges and past numerous country houses, villages, farms, mills and cottages. Rising at Upton on the borders of Berks , below Hurstbourne Park, it is joined by a considerable tributary coming from the north-east and then, after skirting Harewood Forest, at a little below Wherwell, so famed for its trout, it receives the Anton, while some few miles below it passes Stockbridge, the only town of any importance on its banks until it reaches Romsey; some few miles before that happens, so numerous and so wide are the side streams that only one who knows thecountry well can tell which is the Test proper. Though now and again, in times of heavy and prolonged floods, a few salmon will make their way above Romsey and even up as far as Stockbridge, the angling for them is confined almost entirely to the four miles or so of water between Romsey and the tideway. In this distance is comprised the celebrated Broadlands Fishery belonging to the Rt. Hon. Evelyn Ashley ; for not only has it yielded heavy fish and good sport for the past thirty-five years, but it is the nearest salmon angling to the metropolis, which makes it possible for a keen fisher to leave London in the morning, kill his fish, and place it before his friends for dinner that same evening. This four miles of water does not, however, share the features of most other salmon rivers, for the stream flows chiefly in one steady run which is nowhere of any very great depth, while in the shallows the water looks as clear as drinking water in a tumbler when held up to the light, neither are there well- defined pools as they exist in other rivers; nevertheless there are fully thirty named casts, most of them wanting a fairly long line with neat precise casting, for as the river is nowhere very wide the fly is directed more down stream than is usual in larger waters, while it should alight like a snow- flake, at the end of a taut line, so as to be in a position to transact business the moment it is in the water : and many agood angler in the rough and big " catches" of the Scotch rivers will find himself feeling a little awkward when he first attacks the salmon of the Test. The total length is but about thirty-five miles from its source at Upton down to Redbridge, where it falls into the head of Southampton Water, in which distance it drains 446 square miles of country. I believe there still exists an old deed belonging to some Romsey Institution which states that salmon is not to be given to the inmates more than once a week, but to come to. more recent years up to 1861, and prior to that, it was only by chance that salmon ascended as far as Romsey, for the river divided into three streams at the tideway, the southern one being blocked by a fishing mill dam and the other two by fishing weirs, while above these obstacles there was a fresh series of obstructions at Nursling Mill; above this again there was some four miles of open water which had none too much spawning ground, and which was blocked by an impassable weir at Romsey.

Fortunately, however, for the fish, the mills were forced to raise their hatches in times of flood, and in 1860 it was only in this way that salmon got into the river. In 1863 the owners of the fishing weirs agreed to give the fish a jubilee, and neither net nor cruive was worked, while the water above was not fished by rod, for more than two orthree times, though on one of these occasions two rods took seven good fish in the day. Seeing how readily the salmon responded to this act of grace, the owner of the cruive wisely turned it into a fish pass, which was followed by a Meeting of Proprietors being held at Romsey, with the late Lord Palmerston as President, when funds were voluntarily supplied, and it was resolved to place proper fish passes in all the weirs, and to protect the fish in the spawning beds; for the Romsey poachers of those days were a very daring lot. This Association, however, appears to have had but a brief existence, for it was found that the fish passes had not been placed in the run of the fish|that they were liable to be flooded, as they lacked flood-guards|that they were not wide enough, and were much too steep. As no Fishery District for the Test was ever formed, the name of the river has almost disappeared from the Reports of The Fishery Board, and not until 1886 do we find Mr. Berrington visiting the chemical works at Redbridge, where they make sulphuric acid, in order to ascertain that the owner had made perfectly efficient arrangements for avoiding the pollution of the river: then in 1893 Mr. C. E. Fryer visited the river, only to report that "the existing difficulties,"|he does not say what they were| are such as could be more satisfactorily dealt with by aBoard of Conservators. The first serious attempt was made to preserve the river as a salmon angling water in 1881, and in January John Cragg was put on as river keeper, and there he still is, though suffering from failing eyesight; a better one, or a pleasanter or more willing companion, no angler need want. The water above Long- bridge was kept by Lord Mount Temple in his own hands up to the year 1888, while the water below Longbridge down to the Boundary Pool at Nursling was let. Mr. William Clifford, of Magna Charta Island, and Reporter of Chancery Cases for *The Times,* was the first lessee, and he rented the water for seven years, from 1881 up to Lady Day, 1888. Colonel H. Cornwall Legh joined him in the first season, and, taking a warm interest in the Fishery, he brought his experience to bear, and was so tactful in dealing with the mill:hands and the men who managed the water meadows, that, under his guidance, backed by Cragg's vigilance, poaching nearly ceased; the total bag for 1881 was 17 fish in the upper water, averaging 9 Ibs., most of which were taken by Mr. G. R. Kendle, while the lower water yielded 29 fish averaging 10 Ibs. Mr. Clifford died in 1882, and his friend Mr. Basil Field took over the lease in accord with a desire expressed by Mr. Clifford, while he gladly shared it

VOL. I.

with Colonel Legh, and a better sporting partner no man could have. These two then put up a salmon pass| killed the pike, and generally did all they could to improve the water|and thus, though in 1882 the river was very low in May, June, and July, while in October it was continually flooded, they managed to land 44 fish averaging 10 Ibs., while the upper water of Lord Mount Temple yielded but 12 fish of 12f Ibs. average.

1883 was a very good spawning season, and more fish were noticed on the beds near Romsey Mills than had ever been seen before. In June and the two following months the water was very low and bright, which made it impossible to take a proper toll of the large number of salmon in it. Then, in October, angling was stopped on the 7th as the fish had become red unusually early in the season, but, in spite of these drawbacks, the upper water gave up 24 fish and the lower 59, a very satisfactory total of 83 fish, averaging iof Ibs. The first clean fish this season was taken on the 17th March, while on the nth May, Major Dunn killed a 43-pounder in the " South Bend." Also this year Colonel Legh turned in 2,000 Loch Leven yearlings, 1,225 common trout, 4,000 American salmon fry.

1884. A great drought set in at the end of May, and not a fish was caught after the 5th of June. Take fromupper water 13 fish, average i6$ Ibs.; take from lower water 22 fish, average 15 Ibs.

1885. Take from upper water 39 fish, average 13! Ibs. ; take from lower water 70 fish, average 13 Ibs.

1886. First clean fish caught 24th March. On gth April Cragg found a 26-lb. fish dead on the bank of the Boundary

THE COTTAGE STREAM (No. 3 BEAT).

Pool; it had evidently made a bad leap and fallen on dry land, for there was no sign of injury except that the tail was slightly gnawed by rats. June, July and August very low water, during which time Cragg killed a few fish with prawn. The upper water 48 fish, average 12f Ibs.; the lower water 80 fish, average 13 Ibs.

1887. A drought from April to end of season, and the river was at a lower level than had ever been known before, and consequently the estuary nets had an extraordinary good season. A clean fish was caught in the upper water on 26th February, a fortnight earlier than usual. On gth March Colonel Legh had two fish on the lower water of 28 and 24 Ibs., two others on the following day of 22 Ibs. each, and another on the nth of 21 Ibs. Three days of grand sport, for five spring fish averaging 23-fths of a pound is something quite out of the common.

1888. The upper water 20 fish, average 14 Ibs.; the lower water 31 fish, average 15 Ibs. This was the last year of the tenancy of Mr. Basil Field and Colonel Legh, and if the reader will compare the take and average weight of the fish in 1881 with that of 1887 he will see what a remarkable improvement there was; in the seven seasons these two gentlemen and their friends landed 508 salmon, and on one occasion Mr. Basil Field landed six averaging 18 Ibs. before one o'clock. During the three days that I fished this water by the kindness of Colonel Legh, my contribution to this splendid bag was but one clean fish of 12 Ibs. and some fifteen kelts. It blew a gale from the south the whole time and, in spite of Cragg's openly-expressed contempt, I put up a two-inch " Ackroyd," and had there been many cleanfish that lure would have made a record day ; at any rate Cragg was content to beg the fly from me, as he had never seen the pattern before, while, as we parted, he was as emphatic in his praise of it as he had been in his earlier denunciation.

1888. This year the water from "The Shrubbery" to the Boundary Pool at Nursling was let to five rods at $70 each; the tenancy was from 25th March fora year, and each had the right of using, or letting a friend use, a rod on his beat for other fish than salmon. The rods were: Mr. Basil Field and Lord Penrhyn, Col. French and Major Wymer, Col. Griffiths and Sir Charles Larcom, Mr. R. Hargreaves and Lord Winchester, Capt. The Hon. Victor Montagu. The total take was 91 fish, averaging 10 Ibs., and of these just over 20 fell to the rod of Col. French. On the i2th May Mr. T. Jenvey of Romsey caught with a shrimp in Middle Bridge Pool a trout of io$ Ibs., and on the i4th Mr. G. R. Kendle, from the same place and with the same lure, took another of 9 Ibs.lthe brace were stuffed and are still in Mr. Kendle's possession.

1889. This year the angling was let from the Old Ferry to the Boundary at Nursling to six rods at .$80 a rod : they were Col. French and Lord Penrhyn, Col. Griffiths and Mr. Vesey Holt, Mr. R. Hargreaves and Mr. E. Portman,Col. Grant and Mr.

Montagu Guest, Lord Winchester, Mr. Arthur D. Clarke. This, too, was a year of very little rain, and throughout the season the river was below its normal height. On June i4th The Hon. Alan Charteris had a splendid fish of 38 Ibs. on a " Butcher" out of the "Cowman's Hole"; later in the season Col. French had 13 in the last three days of October, though of course here as elsewhere fish are getting a bit off colour at that date. The total take was 103 fish averaging *i* Ibs.

1890. Also a very dry season. Rods : Col. French and Col. Griffiths, Mr. A. Smith and Mr. E. Portman, Col. Grant and Mr. Foster Mortimer, Lord Winchester, Lord Penrhyn, Mr. A. D. Clarke. The heaviest fish of 29 Ibs. was taken by Mr. A. Smith on a "Childers" from the Boundary Pool. On Oct. 3Oth Col. French caught a fish marked on the dorsal fin with a label " T No. i " and the day following another

marked " T No. 2," and both were returned to the river.

1891. Again a very dry season. Rods : Col. Corkran and Hon. Alan Charteris, Lord Penrhyn and Col. French, Col. Grant and Mr. S. Holland, Mr. R. Hargreaves and Sir George Graeme, Mr. F. Mortimer, Lord Winchester. Three of these rods caught 21 trout weighing 68 Ibs., no fish of over 20 Ibs. was captured, the total being 114 averaging io$ Ibs.

1892. A fair supply of water all through the season. Rods: Col. Corkran and Hon. Alan Charteris, Col. Grant and Mr. E. K. Pember. Mr. R. Hargreaves and Sir George Graeme, Mr. F. Mortimer and Mr. C. Walton, Col. A. French and Lord Penrhyn, Earl of Winchester. On the 25th February, Col. French had the first fish, and on the i5th April the heaviest of the season on a " Butcher" from the Cottage Pool which scaled 30 Ibs. Mrs. H. Birkbeck took eight trout weighing 29 Ibs., and at Middlebridge Capt. Streatfield killed with a shrimp on September 2 a trout of ii$ Ibs., which up to this date was the largest ever got in this water. The total take for the season was 130 fish, averaging 14 Ibs., a splendid return ! Up to the end of this year there had been 184 fish killed on the Broadlands private water, and 875 on the section that had been letla total of 1,059 fish weighing 13,295 Ibs., or 5 tons 18 cwts. 79 Ibs. And yet I have heard ignorant people scoff at the Test and say it is not a salmon river !

1893. This was the driest season for many years past, and the fish had scarcely a chance of entering the river. On March gth, Mr. C. Walton had one of 32 Ibs. from the Needle Pool, on a fly with an unpleasant name " The Home Ruler." The total for the season was only 37 fish averaging 13 Ibs. The great drought of this season directed theattention of the anglers to the large quantities of water that were abstracted from the river by the farmers for irrigation purposes, and Cragg was requested to interview some of them with the object of getting them to use less water. Having done so Cragg handed in his report, which is so full of good recommendations that I give it *in extenso,* and it is none the worse or less true if the spelling is somewhat phonetic.

1893.
Broadlands Salmon Fishery In The River Test.

The river been so low during the summer months and the salmon are not able to come up the river and what few do run up will not stop in the lower beats. Owing to the water not been to its proper height and is not fishable and so much complaints with the gentlemen of the water been so low it wood be adviserable to have a regulation on water meadow for the summer months. For farmers to have *all* the water from Novr. up to ist April for watering there meadows and after the ist of April for there sluice atches to be left down from 6 a.m. on Monday morning until 6 p.m. on the Saturday night, and then for the farmers to have all the water from 6 p.m. on Saturday night till 6 a.m. on the Monday morning. And I have no dought that if you could come to this arrangement it would greatly improve the fishing on the lower beats and I have been speaking to some expearance farmers and they say that would be quite sufficant water for any farmer to have and would get much better crop that way than if he was Flooding his meadows night and day. And there should be a proper grating fixed in front of the water meadow atches with small enough of mash so as to prevent the young of salmon from drawing down the meadow as they have been dowing. And also to stop kelts from drawing down after been spawning. For when the man slips the water and sometimes

in m DO U

changes it from one meadow to another the young of the salmon and the kelts are left there to die on the fields. With regard to the netting at the sea, a thing that ought not never to be alowed in such a small river, as it does not give the upper Proprietors a chance for salmon fishing and they have all the trouble of looking after the salmon all the winter in spawning time and there ought to be a Bill brought in by the Government Inspector to stop the netting on a small River like the Test at the mouth of the sea. It also requires a good man to look after the netting at the sea for the summer. And it requires two men hear at Romsey by night to look after the salmon during the time they are spawning on the beds. And one man by day.

1894. Rods: Mr. F. Mortimer and Mr. C. Walton, Gen. French and Col. Grant, R. Hargreaves and Col. Harman, Col. H. Clarke Jervoise, H. Birkbeck, Major Traherne. Thirty- eight pike were destroyed. In May, July and September there was the usual two or three days of weed cutting. Total for season, 65 fish.

1895. Rods the same. They paid ,$75 to two tenants for shutting down the hatches which led to their water meadows for three days in each week. Capt. the Hon. Victor Montagu took the heaviest fish of the season, which weighed 26 Ibs. Total take, 87.

1896. Rods: Col. Clarke Jervoise and Gen. Wygram, Mr. F. Mortimer and Mr. C. Walton, Col. Grant and Col. Harman, Mr. H. Birkbeck, Major Traherne, Mr. R. A. Burrell. Col. Grant had the top weight of the season, with a " Mystery " from the Long Reach, 29 Ibs. Total take, 64 fish.

1897. River high during March and April and a drought from May to end of season. In May Mr. W. Ashley took a trout at Middlebridge of 13 Ibs., which, so far, is the heaviest ever captured, though, in the same month, Mr. Warrender had another of 12 Ibs. Mr. R. A. Burrell had the two heaviest fish, each weighing 24 Ibs. Total take, 46 fish.

Lower down the river comes the Testwood Fishery, belonging to Captain A. P. Beaumont, and which was formerly owned by Colonel Bruce. Part of it is Qn both banks and part on the right bank : its eight or nine pools can all be commanded by a rod of 16 ft. without waders. Bob's Hole, Garden, Warnford, with the three casts below the Bridge, are perhaps the best. March, April and May are the pick of the salmon months ; grilse begin to run in July, while sea trout of from one to seven pounds appear at the end of the month, and these take the " Alexandra" and small salmon flies pretty freely. The average take is about 70 fish per season, though for 1901 and 1902 the average was 107. When the fly proves useless, the prawn will often produce a fish. Captain Beaumont's heaviest weighed 38 Ibs., and all fish are landed with a net and not with a gaff. On the anglings above Testwood the seasons of 1898 and the three following ones were but moderate, and then in 1902 Mr. R. A. Burrell, of Fairthorne Manor, Botley, took thewhole angling, only to experience the worst season ever known on it.

Needless to say the meagre results of the past few seasons naturally attracted the earnest attention of all concerned in the Fishery, with a view of bringing it once more to its former excellence. But though all sorts of theories and suggestions have been put forward, none of them afford any explanation of the phenomenon, for every one of the evils advanced as the cause has been more or less present in the river since 1881. Mr. Douglas Everett who, on Mr. Ashley's behalf, takes the greatest interest in the river, writes me from Broadlands Office that he fears that the tapping of the chalk springs above Romsey by the South Hants Water Company has permanently reduced the volume of water, while also the tenants of the water meadows are now using fully six times as much as they formerly did when the conduits were not kept in such good order. The hatches, moreover, are still unprovided with gratings, and consequently numerous salmon and trout fry die stranded when the water is turned off. Mr. Everett also thinks that the continual dredging that goes on in Southampton Water, and the churning up that it gets by the passing to and fro of the big liners, may also have a prejudicial effect on the fish, and prevent them from making for the head of the estuaryas early as they used to. For the past nine years the owners of the three Salmon Fisheries|Mrs. Vaudrey, Captain Beaumont and Mr. Ashley|have combined together and taken off the nets which the two first-mentioned proprietors have the right of using, each in alternate years, in the tidal water: nevertheless the effect has not been to increase the supply of fish in the river, and in 1891-1892, which were the two best years on it, these nets were in full use. The eel traps at Romsey, moreover, often failed to observe the close time which prohibits them from working between ist December and the 24th June, and at such times they took quantities of smolts which were openly sold in Romsey at 8d. a pound. In this respect a better state of affairs now prevails while poaching from the spawning beds below Romsey is nothing like so rampant as formerly. A good deal of spawn is still destroyed by the town sewage, and by the refuse of tan yards and paper works. There are, likewise, no approved fish passes on the river, but, inasmuch as these have never at any time been perfect, there is not much to be said on that head. As to the fish that ascend above Romsey, the Broadland Fishery has always depended more for its stock of fry from the beds below Romsey than from those above it, though it is undeniable that the more fish that are enabled to ascend to the upper waters the better it must be for the

THE ROOKERY POOL IN BROADLANDS PARK (No. i BEAT).

VOL. I.

river, if the fry are permitted to return to the sea. Thus it would seem as if the diminished number of fish was mainly due to the destruction of their ova by pollution, and to badly constructed fish passes, and that between them they threaten to wipe out the Test as a salmon river yielding first class sport. A vigorous crusade against these two evils would probably speedily restore the river, though it does not lie with me to express an opinion as to whether this would be better done by the Fishery owners or by a Board of Conservators. If legal proceedings were taken against the polluters of the river, good and speedy results might be confidently anticipated. The rod season begins on February ist and ends October 3 ist, and as there is no Board of Conservators, the Test is, I think, the only English salmon river which can be fished without a rod licence, which is a great boon to those anglers who only go to it for one or two days in the season. The following flies have all been often proved to be killers: Wilkinson, Black Dog, Yellow Eagle, Red and Yellow Mystery, Durham Ranger, Silver Grey, Glen Tarra, Ackroyd, Blue and Black Jock Scott, Black and Silver Doctor, Butcher, and Dusty Miller. As they are all standard patterns, there is no need to give their dressings, and if forced into a choice of four, I should take Dusty Miller, Yellow Eagle, Jock Scott and Butcher.

BROADLANDS.

Mr. R. A. Burrell. Major Randolph, And Cracc. Junior, At The Long Bridge Hut.

In coming to the end of my Chapter on the Test there is, perhaps, one other view that may fairly be taken of the decrease, viz. :lthat it is " simply unaccountable," an idea which to some extent is borne out by a conversation I had one day some six years ago on the north coast of Sutherland with one of the most prosperous and largest tacksmen (renter of netting) in Scotland. It was common talk that he had worked at a loss for the last two seasons (and so had the anglers also), but when I condoled with him he merely laughed as he explained that though he could not account for the behaviour of the fish in not coming to the coast in these two seasons, yet his previous experience assured him that they would " make it up in the long run." Three years later we met again, when he told me they " *had* made it uplaye, sir, and a bit more too." To this day the fish have difficulty in passing Testwood, where there are hatches but no mill, while at Nursling Mill the hatches are only opened by one or two at a time, and the force of the water is such that no fish can face the rush, while as to the so- called fish pass, it is more often than not absolutely dry. Now, if really proper and efficient fish passes were put up at Testwood, Nursling, and Romsey, and if the pollutions from that town were done away with, then I think there can be hardly a doubt that this uniquely situated and most sportingriver would speedily regain the famous name which the evils enumerated have obscured for the moment ; so, like my old friend the Scotch tacksman, I venture to prophesy with some confidence that in the near future it will " make it up and a bit more too."

THE BEAULIEU.

Turning to the west out of Southampton Water we soon reach the estuary of this little stream which rises near Lyndhurst in the New Forest, and in times of flood runs porter coloured from peat water. It meets the tideway at Palace House, the residence of Lord Montagu of Beaulieu, who, also owns some three miles of the fresh water of the river with nearly the whole of the estuary, where soles, plaice, bass, mullett, prawns, oysters and wild fowl abound. The stream above the tideway will carry two rods comfortably and can be commanded from the bank by a twelve-foot rod. Hartford Hole is the best catch ; in this part there is a fair quantity of brown trout in the spring, while in June sea trout appear and continue to run till October : fly is the only lure allowed, the favourites being Jock, Butcher, and Silver Doctor dressed on very small double hooks : the last hour of daylight is usually the mostkilling time: the seasons vary. The Honourable John Scott Montagu, the member for the New Forest, the Editor of *The Car* and the popular champion of the motor industry in the House of Commons, took 400 sea trout in one season and then only 100 in the next ; also in about two hours he once caught 13 sea trout which weighed 44 Ibs. ; they ranged from one to ten pounds, the record fish having scaled 12 Ibs. The nets, which are also in Lord Montague's own hands, are rarely used and come off on the ist September; at Beaulieu His Lordship also has a fish hatchery excellently well arranged by Mr. C. Collins.

VOL. I.

2

SECTION 2

Chapter II
  THE AVON AND STOUR
Hampshire

The Avon, which is joined by the Stour at Christchurch, has a course of 67 miles with a catchment basin of 666 square miles. It is formed by the confluence of several small streams above Upavon, and then flowing through the villages of Fittleton, Bulford and Amesbury, it crosses Salisbury Plain, and after skirting the town of the Cathedral with the tall spire it shortly passes Trafalgar House above Downton and then borders the New Forest to Fordingbridge, from which Ringwood is distant about eight miles, while from there to the sea is a further ten. As the Avon drains a chalk country its waters are very clear and neither does it rise or fall with great rapidity, though in times of drought it remains fairly full even when other and larger rivers are reduced to mere trickles. Below Christchurch it expands into a large muddy estuary which eventually contracts into a narrow channel of nearly a mile in length by 70 yards across, and it then discharges into the sea at Muddiford. This channel is calledz
  (i) O
  in

Z O 5
U
X
H

" The Run," and unfortunately for the salmon there is a public right of netting in it. There are two flood tides and only one ebb each day, a phenomenon for which the natives think the Isle of Wight is answerable. It is a very early river which opens for nets and rods on the ist of February, and as its proximity to London easily permits a salmon that has been caught in the morning to make its appearance at the dinner table that same evening, Londoners have made the Christchurch fish famous, and have also pretty well secured a monopoly of them by the high price they are willing to pay for the delicacy. Both the netting and the angling of the river show some remarkable vicissitudes; in 1814 the Knapp or "Royalty" Fishery yielded 1,600 salmon, which take had dwindled to nearly nothing in 1860, and small wonder either, for up to that date a fixed hang net was worked night and day just outside Christchurch Harbour, while another one of some *200* yards was frequently fixed across the river within the Harbour; the total take of these two illegal nets for 1860, '61 and '62 was but 190 fish. Then at about half a mile above the tide point the Knapp Mill fishing dam, called the " Royalty Fishery," formed an almost insurmountable obstacle to the further ascent of fish, as they were netted immediately below it ; the takes at this dam in 1860 were 68 salmon; in 1861, 58 with 250 sea trout; in1862, 73 and 60 sea trout. A short distance above this weir there was another fishing dam at Winkton, and thus these two obstructions practically barred the ascent of fish in any numbers to the spawning beds of the upper waters, until this system of over-netting and obstruction almost ruined a splendid salmon river, on which were, and still are, no pollutions.

Then, at the end of 1862, the fixed nets at the mouth of the river and in the harbour were declared to be illegal ; at the same time fish passes were constructed in the weirs at Knapp and Winkton which gave salmon a better chance of ascending the river up to Ringwood. That this was a step in the right direction was speedily manifest, for early in 1864 there were more breeding fish in the river than had been seen for many years previously, while, in the netting season of

1863, 51 salmon, with a mean weight of i21bs., were taken from a fishery which, up till then, had only averaged six fish a season ; these good results quickly led to the formation of a Fishery Board and an Association, with Earl Nelson as Chairman, when passes were made in the eight weirs above Ringwood, the most important of which were at Burgate, Breumore, and Downton, where Lord Nelson altered the weir at his own expense, so as to make it easily passable. The Avon fish are early spawners, and, with suitable water, mostof the kelts are back in the sea by the end of March|the main netting harvest is in June, with a run of grilse in August. From 1863 the take of the nets gradually increased, until in 1869 those of "The Run" gave a return of 652 fish, as against 40 in 1860, but that did not include the take of the " Royalty Fishery;" therefore, as the owners refused any information, it was assumed that their take was double that of the " Run " nets, which estimate was made, more or less, on hearsay evidence ; though judged by facts that have since been placed at the service of the Conservators, it was probably nothing in excess of the takes of " The Run" nets.

As soon as the Avon was opened up a new difficulty presented itself in the complicated system of irrigation, the water being taken from the main stream by large cuttings, divided into smaller ones, which were again subdivided, until at last they became rills of barely a foot in width ; from these narrow channels no fish could escape, except by overflow, and thus as the smolts and kelts entered them freely in their descent to the sea, their destruction was inevitable ; the evil, however, was met by a system of rewards and payments to the " drowners," or watermen, who attended to the irrigation, and by this method many wanderers were ensured a careful removal and return to the main stream.

The following table of takes to nets and rods from 1869 will show the fluctuations to which the river has been subject:|

Take by Nets Take by Rods Number of
exclusive of exclusive of Rod Licences
Royalty Fishery Royalty Fishery. at 203. each.
1869 768 ... ... 10 ii
1870 774 ... ... No record 16
1871 1,060 ... ... No record.
1872 445 (one of 42 Ibs.) 17
1873 1,046 9 19
1874 358 14 19
11875 648 ... ... 13 on Ringwood Water ... 14
1876 565 39 34
1877 413 100 36
1878 368 (one of 47 Ibs.) ... 25 43
1879 537 36 (one of 48 Ibs.) ... 33
1880 717 ... ... 28 23
1881 763 40 (average 21 Ibs.) ... 37
1882 1,017 155 (average 19 Ibs.) ... 73
1883 1,714 168 92
1884 1,294 ... ... 221 83
1885 957 (one of 40 Ibs.) ... 132 (one of 41 Ibs.) ... 78 + 1886 Fishery Board Report not procurable.
1887 1,544 155 93
1888 806 72 (average 18 Ibs.) ... 71

The take of the Royalty Fishery can be put down as equal to the total take of all the others.

t Close time curtailed from 1st September to 151)1 August, and weekly close time extended from 42 to 48 hours.

J " In this year a pike was taken which had been choked in the endeavour to swallow a salmon of loj Ibs. The weight of the pike has not reached me."

(Signed) A. D. Berrington.

Take by Nets Take by Rods Number of
exclusive of exclusive of Rod Licences

Royalty Fishery Royalty Fishery. at 205. each.

1889 644 ... ... no 55
1890 321 ... ... 17 70
1891 757 n 63
1892 1,012 ... ... 40 93
1893 486 ... ... 22 85
1894 916 55 75
1895 i39 " 25 ... - 63
1896 1,039 28 73
1897 459 ... ... 62 87
1898 605 31 65
1899 522 ... ... 40 95
tigoo 235 38 76
1901 386 13 43
i92 355 23 44

The netting returns for 1902 are not yet to hand, but it is not probable that they will show any improvement, as the number caught by the rods was very small. In the early part of February Mr. T. Kingston Barton, with several other anglers, marked all the kelts they caught by cutting off a piece of the tail on the top side. On February 3rd Mr. Barton marked six kelts in this way. On April 2nd Mr. Reginald Morant landed a clean fish of 28 Ibs. with a tail mutilated as described, which he sent to Mr. Barton, who was nearly positive that it was one of the six that hehad marked himself, none of which were over 17 Ibs. This tends to confirm the correctness of the history of the capture offish " D. 1502," which was caught in February in the Shannon, and weighing 19 Ibs. was marked as above; it was recaught only 34 days later as a clean spring fish of 33 Ibs., with the same label attached to it. There have been, however, a few other marked kelts caught in the Avon, which were only retaken after the lapse of a year. The chief proprietors of the river above Ringwood, where salmon are seldom seen except in the late autumn, are the Earl Nelson at Downton, Sir Edward Hulse at Breamore, and Lord Normanton at Somerley. Below Ringwood the owners are Mr. E. Morant, the Manor House, Ringwood, the Rev. Cecil Mills of Bisterne Park, Lord Manners at Avon Tyrell, Mr. Fane of Moyles Court, and Miss Mills at Christchurch, who has the Winkton and Knapp fisheries. Mr. Mills owns the Bisterne water, extending about three miles, which is a " Royalty" fishery comprising the actual ownership of the river bed, while, lower down, Miss Mills owns the Winkton water for some two miles below Sopley, which is also a " Royalty " affair; in some years both these waters are kept in the hands of their owners, while at others they are let to single tenants. Half-a-mile of this water is usually let to the tenant of Avon Castle, and in the days when my old friendMr. Turner-Turner owned this charming place, which is on the right bank of the river at the top of the Bisterne section, he also rented the rest of it as well as the whole of the Avon Tyrell water belonging to Lord Manners, a total length of seven miles, which in 1896 yielded but eight fish ; the heaviest, weighing 35 Ibs., falling to the rod of Mr. Cooper; in 1897 fifteen were caught, one of 20 Ibs. being landed by Mr. Turner-Turner ; in 1898 twelve were taken, one of 39 Ibs. by Mr. Turner-Turner and one of 34 Ibs. by Mr. Cooper ; in 1899 nineteen were brought to bank, a thirty-two-pounder by Mr. Turner-Turner, and one of 29 Ibs. by Mr. R. N. Knatchbull; in 1900 only ten were accounted for, and none of them over 30 Ibs. ; then at the end of that season Mr. Turner-Turner sold Avon Castle.

The passes at the " Royalty " and Winkton were found to have become defective. t In this and in future years the take includes that of the " Royalty."

Below Ringwood the water belongs to Mr. E. T. Morant of Dilton, Brockenhurst: it is known as the " Ringwood Water " and consists of two-and-a-half miles of the left bank, and is let by ticket from the " White Hart " Hotel at 5$. a day to those who stay there and at *js. 6d. a* day to those who do not. Rod licence is *205.* There are thirteen named casts in this section : Brigand's Hole, The Farm, The Firs, Pollard Tree, The Larder, The Piles, Bend, Big Hole and Gaspipe being perhaps the best. Wading trousers are not necessary, as stockings and an i8-ft. rod will be all that isneedful. March and April are the best months for spring fish, for after May the winds prevent angling, and though it has been tried it has been found that the fish will rarely take anything. The best flies are Yellow and Grey Eagle, Popham, Durham Ranger, Mystery, with black and silver Doctor : baits are not permitted until ist of May, when the best are prawn and gudgeon. A gaff may be carried from the opening day, but, of course, all kelts are tailed and returned. Since 1892 this water has given an average of 17 fish per season with a mean weight of 23- Ibs., sometimes more and rarely less. There are no grilse and more than a fish a day seldom happens, though Mr. Campbell had three in one day with bait in 1902 and Mr. R. M. H. Morant two in a day, one with fly, the other with bait; many heavy fish have been captured, and in recent times Mr. Turner-Turner had one of 44 Ibs. and another of 39 Ibs., Mr. Lewis had one of 42 Ibs., Mr. Aldin one of 40 Ibs., Mr. R. Morant one of 38 and Mr. Campbell one of 37. There are no sea trout and no one can foretell what will be a good day for salmon, as they have been caught in all sorts of weather. Close times at present are: for nets from 3ist July to ist February, for rods from 2nd October to ist February.

Chairman of Board of Conservators: The HonourableE. B. Portman, 46, Cadogan Place, London. *Clerk to Board:* Mr. H. Symonds, Christchurch, Hants.

THE STOUR

Rises in Wiltshire at Stourhead and, shortly passing into Dorsetshire, it flows through that county for upwards of fifty miles ere it enters Hampshire near Parley village, from whence it has a further run of some eleven miles before it joins the estuary of the Avon at Christchurch; the chief places of interest on its banks are Gillingham, Sturminster Newton, Blandford, Corfe Mullen and Wimborne, while the largest proprietors are Viscount Portman at Bryanstone Park, Lord Wimborne at Canford Manor, and the Earl of Malmesbury at Heron Court, who have spared no pains to make the Stour into a productive salmon river. Though originating in a chalk district the stream is slow and sluggish, and somewhat muddy, and it is curious to see the difference in the colour of the water at the junction with the clear- flowing Avon, for after a flood the Stour remains dirty for fully a fortnight, while the Avon clears itself in two or three days; then about the end of May the river-bed becomes matted with rushes and weeds to such an extent as to almostprevent fish from ascending : in 1873 Lord Malmesbury cut a way through these impediments from Wick right up to

Throop Weir, when a fish of 36 Ibs. was killed with the rod in the pool below it, which was the first fish ever caught there by an angler. Pike also abound and devour great

THE JUNCTION AT CHRISTCHURCH.

numbers of smolts each season. The waterman at Ham Mill near Canford, prior to 1865, had frequently seen fish spawning at the Mill tail, but after that date he had observed more. Then in 1872, which was a very wet year, salmon were seen at Spettisbury some forty miles up the river, the continual floods having enabled them to surmount theobstacles offered to their passage by the weirs at Throop, Long Ham, Canford, Corfe Mullen and Whitehill, and between Throop and Spettisbury lie the best spawning grounds, as the poachers know only too well ; if the fish had a perfectly free access to these reaches, and were efficiently protected, there is no doubt that the number of salmon would be greatly increased.

In 1874 only nine fish were netted; by 1880 the take had increased to twenty-two, while in January, 1885, twenty- three fish that had died of disease were removed from the river, and in the Spring following, larger numbers of salmon were observed to pass up than had ever been previously known, while the very early runners seemed to prefer the Stour to the Avon. In 1887, Lord Malmesbury put a fish pass in Throop weir, which, however, was of faulty construction, and failed to answer expectations ; passes were also constructed on the other weirs above Throop, but as they were on the same principle, none of them were of much use, and though, since then, alterations have been made, they yet remain anything but perfect. Lord Malmesbury's fishings extend from I ford Dowles, which is a little way from the junction, up to the County march below Redhill, a distance of about eight miles, almost entirely on the left bank, and the greater part of the right one. Unless a boat is used, waders are

VOL. I.

required for many of the pools, while others can be fished from the bank. The best catches are a little above and a little below the weirs at Throop, and a little below Blackwater Ferry, though fish lie more or less along the whole stretch. The close times are the same as those for the Avon, viz., opening for rods and nets on February ist, and closing for the latter on the ist August, and for the former on the 2nd October. From the opening day to the end of April is the best time, and neither grilse nor sea trout enter the river. The rod licence is *2os.,* and a gaff may be carried from the opening day, though it is expected that kelts will be tailed, and returned uninjured. The Eagles, yellow and grey, with Jock Scott and Thunder and Lightning, dressed large on hooks 4/0 to 6/0, are the favourite flies, while prawn and spoon are also used. Fish average 2 if Ibs., though Cameron, the head keeper, has had one of 40 Ibs., and Mr. H. E. Gilbert another of 36 Ibs. The best take made in recent years on this Heron's Court water has been 96 fish in one season, but this was made by net as well as by rod. As the Earl does not fish, he sometimes lets the angling. There is no Hotel water on the Stour.

D

O

Ui
la

X
H

Z
O

of
u

X
H

3

SECTION 3

Chapter 111
THE FROME

This river is also a chalk stream for the greater part of its 34 mile course, in which it drains 206 square miles : it must not be confounded with the Somersetshire one of the same name that joins the Avon which flows into the Bristol Channel, for it is wholly a Dorsetshire river, formed by the junction of two streams at Newton some seven miles above the County town of Dorchester, between which place and Wareham there is a further fifteen miles, and then two miles lower down the Frome falls into one of the bays of Pool Harbour. Prior to 1866 there was a bar net drawn right across the river at Wareham which stopped the ascent of nearly every fish, while the few that escaped in times of floods were caught in fixed engines at the weirs of East Stoke and Brindon Abbey Mills. At that date the salmon were almost wiped out, though it is recorded in the old chronicles of Dorset that a century earlier they were so numerous that the officials of Wareham made a law that the apprentices of that town were not to be fed more than three times a weekon salmon. In 1867 a Board of Conservators was formed, with the late Mr. Charles Hambro of Milton Abbey as Chairman, and the river at once began to show signs of improving, for he took the matter up warmly and raised sufficient annual subscriptions to pay for a water bailiff and give rewards to the " drowners" or watermead men for

THE FROME AT WAREHAM.

removing fish and fry and carrying them back to the main stream ; Mr. Hambro also started a hatchery, while Colonel Napier Sturt followed his good example. At first the owner of the Stoke Weir, Sir Henry Oglander (title now extinct) refused permission to place a pass in it, but when Mr. Weldof Lul worth Castle at once consented to have one placed in the Bindon Abbey Weir his further opposition was withdrawn ; unfortunately both these passes were so badly placed as to be practically useless and, as before, the few fish that got over them only did so when the water was suitably high : better preservation, however, soon began to tell, and the history of the river from that period may be gathered from the following statistics :|

1868. 20 salmon netted ; no rod used.

1869. 27 netted, average 9 Ibs., first fish caught 3ist May; no rod used.

1870. 31 netted; no rod used.

1871. 45 netted ; i rod licence issued.

1872. 14 netted, average io$ Ibs.; no rod licence.

1873. 46 netted; no rod licence.

J874- 33 netted ; no rod licence issued.

1875. 40 netted, average 10 Ibs; no rod licence issued.

1876. No record.

1877. 14 netted, average 12 Ibs; 2 rod licences: the first fish caught with the rod weighed 25 Ibs.

1878 to 1891. No record. In 1899 there were n rod licences issued, so presumably there were a good few fish taken.

1892. 60 netted; 20 to rod; 5 licences.

VOL. I.

- 5 netted, average 25 Ibs. ; 20 to rod, average 15 Ibs. ; 7 licences.

1894. No record.

1895. IO5 netted; 5 to rod; 6 licences.

1896. 51 netted; 3 to rod of 16 Ibs. average; 3 licences.

1897. No record.

1898. 37 netted, average 20 Ibs. ; 2 to rod, average 25 Ibs. ; 5 licences.

1899. 21 netted; 8 to rod, average 26 Ibs.; n licences.

1900. 6 netted ; i to rod, 26 Ibs. ; 9 licences.

1901. 5 netted; 2 to rod, 16 Ibs. each; 4 licences

1902. No report; 9 licences.

The increase of weight is a remarkable feature of these statistics, for in 1869, 27 fish averaged but 9 Ibs. ; in 1875 40 others averaged 10 Ibs., and then in 1893, on"y eighteen years later, we find 50 netted fish averaged 25 Ibs. and 20 rod fish averaged 15 Ibs. Presumably 1895 was a very dry year, for though the nets took 105 fish I a record catch I yet six rods are reported to have only got five fish between them.

In the time of the late Mr. Charles Hambro, he and Mr. Montague Guest rented the greater part of the river, which then came in for much attention, which well repaidthem for their trouble, as quite decent bags were made. The tide from Pool Harbour affects the stream for several miles upwards and spoils it for angling, though this part was incessantly netted up to about twenty years ago, and as many as 150 fish are said to have been scooped out in one season by netting the pools when the river was low. Though the fish have access to a long stretch of the river they seldom or ever ascend above the top of the Lulworth Estate, which is only about twelve miles above the mouth, and then only in the spawning season. The various river owners from the mouth up, are: on the South Bank, Mr. Marsden, the Earl of Eldon, Mr. N. Bond of Creech Grange, Mr. W. H. Hudle- stone of West Holme, and Mr. Weed of Lul worth Castle, while on the North Bank there is Mrs. Erle-Drox of Charl-. borough Park, Lord Alington, and Captain J. Fyler of Hethfelton. For the last few years the river has been steadily declining, and now it has fallen so low that it is not considered worth netting at the mouth. It is a difficult matter to explain, but in the opinion of Captain E. C. Radclyffe, of Hyde, Wareham, who has known and fished the river for many years, it is owing partly to the formation of a big mud bank across the mouth of the river in Pool Harbour, and while the river is very gradually cutting a new channel for itself, the fish are retarded by this obstacle; also the river

has become very foul with masses of weed, which are not now cut as frequently as they used to be in the days of Mr. Hambro, and salmon appear to dislike pushing their way up through these weeds, and so they hang back until they die down in the autumn, when they come up to spawn, Captain Radclyffe says that in this February of 1903 there are more fish on the spawning beds than for many years past. Another drawback is that the river is literally swarming with coarse fish, amongst which are heavy pike, with a good few otters on the banks; his opinion is that scarcely any fry hatched in the river ever live to get to the sea, and that that is the explanation of the absence of grilse, for there are nothing but heavy old fish which average about 30 lbs. each. Captain Radclyffe once caught a fish of 12 lbs., when his keeper, who had never seen any other salmon river, at once wanted to know "what kind of a fish the little brute was?" In 1898 and 1899, Captain Radclyffe and Mr. J. Spiller rented the best and greater part of the angling, and, taking some trouble to improve it, it began to show signs of mending, for in '99 Captain Radclyffe had seven fish which averaged within a fraction of 30 lbs. each; then the war in South Africa claimed him and the river was scarcely fished, so that in 1902 not a single fish was killed by the rod in the whole water.

The trout fishing of the river is something unique, for Captain Radclyffe has caught as many as 50 brace in a day, using only one fly, and though the fish do not run very heavy he has had them up to 3 lbs. The record fish was taken about twelve years ago by Mr. S. Osborne, and weighed 46 lbs. The river is a small one, about thirty yards wide; there are nice streams in the upper waters, though the lower reaches are somewhat canal-like. Early in the season big flies up to size 5/0 Limerick hooks are used, Grey and Yellow Eagle with Jock Scott and Black Doctor are the favourites, though later on when the weather is bright and water clear nothing is used but the "Yellow Mystery," made specially for Captain Radclyffe by Farlow, size 2/0; also the Childers, and sometimes the prawn, is also very killing. There are plenty of pools almost in every place wherever the river makes a bend, the three best perhaps being "

The Boundary Stone," Drax's Pool, and Bond's Pool, while there is room for four or five rods in the eight miles of the best water. April, May, and the early part of June is the season.

There are no rules as to carrying a gaff, but anglers always tail their kelts. There is rather a good yarn told by the old water bailiff, John Marsh of Wareham, who swears that on one occasion, several years ago, a gentleman (if mymemory is right, Admiral Baird) hooked and played a fish, which finally got fast in weeds in very deep water, and as it grew dark they cut the line, and tying Marsh's hat to it, they threw it into the river; the next morning they came up from Wareham in a boat to prospect, and found the hat with the fish still fastened to it, so the line was gently tied to the reel and the patient captive duly landed.

Nets fish from ist February to ist September; rods from ist February to 2nd November; rod licence *2os.*

Chaiiman of Board of Conservators: Mr. G. D. Bond, East Holme, Wareham. *Clerk to Board:* Mr. P. E. L. Budge, Wareham.

4

SECTION 4

Chapter IV
THE AXE

With a total course of some twenty miles and draining 165 square miles, rises in Dorset and in about eight miles passes into Somerset at Clopton Bridge at Seaborough, to form the march between the two counties until, on reaching Holditch, it enters Devon, when about six miles further on it passes through Axminster, to be joined by the Yarty river a little distance below, while in a further six or seven miles it forms a narrow estuary of about two miles in length. In 1862 the river was fished out by mackerel seines which worked at the mouth and captured nearly every fish, while even if they escaped the further dangers of the nets in the river itself they were brought to a standstill by Axminster Weir, from below which they were netted. In those days a few salmon used to enter the estuary as early as April, when, together with the kelts and the fry, they were quickly netted, and at that time everyone fished, how, when and where he pleased. In 1868 Mr. Buckland reported that the AxminsterWeir some 16 miles above the tideway was the chief obstruction in the river, though there were other bad weirs above it at Weycroft and Cooxden, and he expressly stated that if salmon were enabled to ascend them they would be made welcome and carefully preserved by

Mr. Evens of Forde Abbey, Lord Bridport, Lord Paulet and other upper Proprietors. The Yarty is also a fine spawning stream, though at this period the Westwater Weir was nearly a total obstruction. Grilse, bull trout and sea trout ran in July and August, and salmon followed in September and the next two months; in this year of 1868 twenty-three anglers thought it worth while to take out rod licences at 20. each. Though salmon did not enter the river till September they congregated in the estuary as early as July, in which month the nets took 30 cwts. of *salmonida.*

In 1869 there were 19 rod licencees, who took 5 salmon between them, all after the end of August.

In 1872 10 licences took 30 grilse and sea trout, but no salmon.

1873. A pass was placed in Westwater Weir on the Yarty, while simultaneously the proprietors above Axminster protested that they did not wish for salmon to be passed into their waters, as they feared their presence would spoil their trout fishings, which were quite excellent. Mr. F. Swabey of

CE Ul

Coryton Park caught in one August day 5 grilse above West- water Weir.

1874. The nets took 5 salmon and 200 grilse and sea trout; 14 rod licences taken outlno takes reported.

1875. Nets took 14 cwt. of *salmonicUe* 14 rod licences reported.

1876. Nets took 7 salmon, 425 grilse and peal; 4 rod licencees took 2 sea trout.

1877. 3 rod licencees got 23 peal.

1878. Nets took 14 salmon and 2,300 Ibs. of grilse and peal; 2 rod licencees took 10 peal.

1879. Nets took 14 salmon, total 108 Ibs. and 1890 Ibs. of peal; 2 rod licences.

1880. Nets took 25 salmon and 1,70x5 Ibs. of peal; 3 rod licences.

1881. Nets took 15 salmon and 1,500 Ibs. of peal; only one rod licence.

1882. Nets took 2 salmon and 1880 Ibs. peal; 3 rod licences.

1883. 5 rod licencees took 13 peal.

1884. Nets took 30 salmon averaging 8 Ibs. and 2,960 Ibs. of peal; 5 licencees took 20 sea trout averaging 3 Ibs.

1885. Nets took 60 salmon and 2,220 Ibs. of peal; 5 rod licences. No report.

1886. Nets took 45 salmon and 650 peal; 8 rod licences.

No report.

1887. Nets took 78 salmon and 1253 trout; 4 rod licences.

1888. Nets took 40 salmon and 2,100 Ibs. of peal; 8 rod licences.

1889. No reports; only 2 rod licences. The fishing much damaged by the capture of fry and kelts by seine nets of small mesh in the estuary.

1890. Rod licence reduced from 20. to *los.*

no reports.

1891. Rodlicences 331892. 361893- 341894. 27t895- ..281896. 261897- .. 261898. 221899- 251900. 211901. 121902. 17From the foregoing it will be seen that the Axe is not a river that would be specially selected by an angler comingfrom a distance to seek sport with salmon and sea trout only. A study of the number of the salmon rod licences issued each season will convince anyone on that point. For those, however, who are content with fair trouting, with an occasional chance of a salmon or a peal, the Axe holds out undoubted attractions, and that there is a good stock of trout in its course of twenty miles, is evidenced by the fact that in 1901 no less than 144 licences at *2s. 6d.* each were issued. The close time for nets is from 20th September to ist May, and for rods from 20th November till ist May.

The *Chairman of the Board of Conservators* is Mr. W. H. B. Knight, of Hilary House, Axminster. *Clerk to Board:* Mr. W. Forward, Axminster.

THE OTTER

Flows for some 25 miles, with a catchment basin of 95 square miles, entirely through Devonshire ; for, rising on the borders of Somerset, it flows mainly due south, past Honiton and Ottery St. Mary, to expand at Otterton some seven miles lower down into a small estuary with Budleigh Salterton at its mouth. From Otterton to the mouth is a distance of three miles, of which two are tidal, and at Otterton Weir,fish formerly met with the first obstruction in the shape of a trap in the mill weir ; three miles above there was another weir at Tipton, with several others beyond it. Prior to 1863, when a Board of Conservators was formed, there was no protection worthy of mention, for the Axe estuary, like all

THE OTTER AT OTTERTON.

the other rivers of Devon, offered to netters the very greatest facilities for the capture of clean fish, kelts, and smolts.

In 1866 Mr. Buckland reported that "all obstacles to the ascent of salmon have now been removed, and the River Otter has been, during close time, full of salmon, which has not been known before for forty years."

In 1867 Mr. Walpole visited the river and reported: " This river was at one time strictly preserved, and a capital brown trout river. This fish runs to a large size, and salmon remain for so short a time in the Otter that less attention was paid than might have been, owing to fine quality trout. Unfortunately, a few years ago some of the landowners withdrew from the Association which was protecting the river; since then it has been terribly poached, and the pools which were once full of fish are almost depopulated. I was present in September at a meeting at Ottery St. Mary, which I am in hopes will lead to a better state of things, as it is lamentable to see a river of such considerable spawning capabilities so neglected as the Otter."

As it happened, however, neither the sanguine report of Mr. Buckland or the depressing one of Mr. Walpole were destined to end in satisfactory results. In 1886 the Honble. Mark Rolle, the owner of the river from Budleigh Salterton to Ottery St. Mary, agreed to abandon his fishing weir and trap at Otterton, while in 1888 he threw open to the public this ten miles of river. By this date the Board had ceased to exist, and no further mention of the Otter as a salmon river is made in the Reports of the Fishery Inspectors. The attempt to make it into a salmon angling river was a failure, " and we trust that it never will be one, for it is one of the

VOL. I.

best trout streams in the West of England " is the emphatic verdict of the riparian owners. It may be mentioned that the trout licence is *is.* ; season from February ist to August 31 st. Applications for leave to fish between Ottery St. Mary and the Mouth should be made to the Agent at Bicton.

There are, however, still a few peal killed in the Otter, and for that reason I have not liked to pass it by unnoticed. Also, it may be doubted whether the fear of the proprietors lest the presence of salmon should destroy their trout fishing is well grounded, for the Usk and the Don are both celebrated trout streams, indeed, there are hardly any better ones, and yet they both hold salmon in large numbers.

5

SECTION 5

Chapter V
THE EXE

Rises in Exe Head Hill, in the West of Exmoor Forest, in Somerset, and, after a run of about fifteen miles, it is joined by the Barle at Dulverton Station, where it enters Devon; thence, passing by Stoodleigh, Tiverton and Bickleigh, it winds its way past Brampford Speke to Exeter, shortly opening out into a large estuary of some seven miles in length, with Exmouth at the sea end. A few miles above Exeter the Culm falls in on the left bank and the Greedy on the right. As it has a course of some sixty miles, during which it receives many smaller tributaries, and drains 584 square miles, it will be seen that the Exe is a good sized river, fully capable of holding a large quantity of *salmonicUe*. In 1862 they were, however, in a fair way to be wiped out, for in the estuary there were quite one hundred boats working small-mesh Seine nets of 120 yards in length, while they fished regardless of close time, capturing salmon, keltsand smolts whenever they could, while if any breeding fish escaped to make their way into the river they were met by a succession of weirs which they could only ascend in times of flood. In the two miles immediately above the tideway there were no less than five of these weirs ; the Salmon Pool Weir was the nearest to the sea, and worked a paper mill; then the Exeter Town Council owned the next three weirs, one of which, " The Countess Weir," is said to have been built by order of the Countess de Redvers in the i6th century, when she cut Exeter off from the sea for defensive purposes ; the fifth is the Cowley Bridge Weir, put up by the Bristol and Exeter Railway Company ; and above these there are fully half-a-dozen others, all of which at that time offered more or less hindrance to the free passage of fish. Therefore, when in 1862 a Board of Conservators was formed, the two first matters to which they turned their attention was the placing of fish passes in those weirs, and to seeing that the poisonous refuse from the four paper mills was so disposed of as to do no further harm. Also in the winter of this year 104 salmon were lifted by the water bailiffs over one of the weirs, and another 54 were carried up Cowley Weir, and so the good work went steadily on, until in 1867 the Salmon, or Tames Weir, Trew's Weir, Blackaller Weir, and the Countess Weir were declared to be no longer a barto the ascent of fish, and attention was directed to the weirs higher up at Pynes, Thorverton, and Bickley. In this year the nets caught about 300 fish, and the only two rods that were licensed took under a dozen between them.

In 1868 and 1869 fish passes were still being made and bettered.

In 1870 there was a renewal of pollution. Only one rod licence was taken out at "*js. 6at.,* and the holder caught nothing!

It was reported by the bailiffs that the fishermen netted the sand banks at Topsham nightly, and that if they were present the men threw salmon back to the water, previously injuring them in such a manner that they would die and be easily recovered later on, while if the bailiffs were not there, all fish were killed and hidden for future removal.

1871. No returns of netting ; no fish killed by rod.

1872. No returns of netting ; two or, perhaps, three fish caught by rod.

1873. No returns of netting; i rod licence issued at "*js. 6d.* Pollutions still very bad.

1874. 5 rod licences issued; no returns of nets or rods.

1875. About 3,000 fish netted, of which 600 were caught by the middle of May; 5 rod licences issued, and 2 salmon were caught by the rod above Head Weir.

VOL. I.

1876. About ,$1,000 worth of fish netted ; 20 rod licences issued at *js. 6d.*

1877. About ,$1,000 worth of fish netted, weighing 9,000 Ibs.; 32 rod licences issued and 70 salmon taken by them.

1878. No reports available. At this period the close time for nets was from 3ist August to ist February; for rods from November ist to ist February.

1879. Nets took 7,700 Ibs. of salmon; 93 rod licences at *2os. ;* 100 salmon were taken by them.

1880. 105 salmon taken by the rods of 57 licencees.

1881. Nets took 350 salmon, and 34 rod licencees took 70 salmon.

1882. 81 rod licencees took 400 fish weighing 2,000 Ibs.

1883. 68 rod licencees took 300 salmon.

1884. 76 rod licencees took between 250 and 280 fish, weighing 2,200 Ibs. A distinct increase observed in the average weight of salmon.

1885. A very dry season; 76 rods took 120 fish.

1886. Also a dry season ; 74 rods took 120 fish.

1887. A very dry season ; 25 rods took 55 fish.

1888. An average season; 50 rods took 120 fish.

1889. A dry season; 22 rods took 55 fish. Trout licences were made compulsory in this year ; there were 639of these issued at *2s. 6d.* and 304 day licences at *is.:* total, "95. *is. 6d.*

1890. 60 rods took 200 fish averaging 8 Ibs.

1891. 53 rods took 300 fish averaging 8 Ibs. Monthly licences at *js. 6d.* were introduced.

1892. 30 rods took 80 fish.

1893. A very dry season ; 28 rods took 40 fish.

1894. Nets took 1,613 salmon; 33 rods took 116 fish.

1895. Nets took 1,747 fish; 25 rods took 139.

1896. Nets took 1,200 fish; 31 rods took 121 fish.

1897. Nets took 1,000 fish ; 46 rods took 155 fish averaging nearly 10 Ibs. each.

1898. Nets took 2,205 fish; 53 rods took 112 fish. The cost of a rod licence taken out after the end- of June was reduced to *i2s. 6a.*

1899. Nets took 2,526 fish; 46 rods took 115 fish. Complaints were made that the river was over-netted in the tidal waters and in the river itseli.

1900. Nets took 1,704 fish; 34 rods took 50 fish.

1901. Nets took 3,106 fish; 38 rods took 125 fish. These returns show very clearly how greatly a good

Board of Conservators can improve the angling of a river without in any way injuring its productiveness as a netting one. In 1875 3,000 fish were netted, while the 5 rodlicencees caught but 2 salmon. In 1901 we find that though the nets took 3,106 fish, 38 rod licence holders took 125 fish. There is no doubt that the Exe is one of the very best managed rivers in England or Wales.

1902. A very dry spring. Nets took 3,242 fish, while comparatively very few were got by the rods, and those quite late in the season l77 fish weighing 750 Ibs.; of these few Captain Lupton on Up-Exe had 11 fish, averaging 9 Ibs. In 1884 the Board of Conservators purchased the netting rights in the Salmon Weir at the top of the tideway, and, ceasing to net, they let the angling in 1887 to Mr. R. N. Baker, and thus the nets at Trew's and Countess Weir are the only nets in the river itself, though the estuary is fished by an average of 26 nets per season. The nets at Trew's Weir were not started until 1886, which was after the removal of the nets of the Salmon Pool Weir below it, and though the Conservators then tried to purchase these nets also, the negotiations fell through. The Salmon Pool Fishery extends for about a mile on both banks, and has been held by Mr. R. N. J. Baker of Heavitree for the last sixteen years ; it is the property of the Earl of Devon, who lets it to the Exe Conservators; there are four principal pools and one or two " bitties," which are cast from the bank or reached by wading stockings ; their names are Double LocksRun, Doctor's Pit, the Run, and the Weir Pool, and they will give employment to two rods every day when they are in order. The spring tides flow right up to Salmon Pool Weir, and as the fish will not look at a fly, they are all caught on a Devon minnow and a i4-ft. spinning rod. The best months are March with April, but the use of the gaff is prohibited before the i5th March and during the month of October. Mr. Baker's best season has been 67 salmon weighing 643 Ibs. ; his worst was 4 salmon averaging 8 Ibs. After the i5th May fishing in this section is almost a waste of time. On April 4th, 1888, Captain Pretyman, M.P. had 7 fish of 9 Ibs. each. On March 2nd, 1896, Messrs. Baker and J. Moysey had 8 fish of nearly n Ibs. each. The four largest fish taken here have all fallen to the rod of Mr. Cecil Baker, 30 Ibs., 22 Ibs., 22 Ibs. and 20 Ibs., while on 4th March, 1899, he landed and of course returned a kelt of 40 Ibs., the largest fish ever seen in the river. There are so few sea trout that it may almost be said there are none at all.

The angling of Trew's Weir is on the right bank and consists of only one stream not many yards in length ; it is netted after the 1510 March, but nevertheless yields a fish or two each season to the Devon minnow ; it is rented by Mr. C. Coleridge of Old Abbey, the Chief Constable ofDevon. Above this comes the water of the Lower Exe Angling Association, extending for about three miles, from Cowley Bridge to Brampford Speke ; on this section the fly kills well, while minnow and worm are also successful bait lures, the latter for choice ; above this section is Mr. Hill's private water and then, higher up again, is the Collipriest water of Mr. C. Carew. The Up-Exe Angling Association contains some three miles of water on which fly only may be used until May ist, while on the lands of Mr. Troyte of Huntsham Court fly is compulsory all the season. Above this comes the Tiverton Angling Association, which is trout fishing only, the salmon angling being reserved by the Messrs. Carew. On this water, yearly tickets for trouting with artificial fly only are issued at 3.; Mr. H. Mudford, Fore Street, Tiverton, issues them, as well as others for shorter periods. The water extends upwards for about 3 miles above Tiverton on the left bank only, but, as wading is allowed, the other side is easily commanded. Below the Town the Association has another 3 miles on both banks. The head weir at Tiverton except in times of flood offers a great bar to the ascent of salmon, and it is still a subject of dispute with the Board of Trade. As trout have decreased grayling have increased. The best flies are Silver Doctor, Infallible, Durham Ranger and Silver Grey,

3 O I

0.

UJ

Jock Scott, Butcher, and Eagles, while for trout the Blue Upright, Red Upright, Halfstone, Grannom, Iron Blue and March Brown are best: trout have been on the decline for some years past and no attempt has been made at restocking, while poaching is pretty bad. North winds are the worst though an Easterly one is good after the second day, while South and Westerly winds are the best. Perhaps also the pike bred in the Exeter Canal, into which they were unfortunately introduced some years since, may have a good deal to say to the trout decline, for though these pests do not run large they are very numerous, the water bailiff having killed close on eighty of them last season. The Up-Exe Fishing Association is only for trout, and members cannot fish for salmon without the permission of the occupiers of the lands, of whom there are just ten. The season is from ist March to 3ist August with a 7 inch limit. No wading allowed till ist May, after which date minnow may be used, and also the worm after i6th June to end of August. This does not apply to the lands of Mr. H. A. Troyte of Huntsham Court. Season tickets, 315-. *6d.* ; half-season from 2nd May, 21.; monthly, 15.; weekly, *75. 6d. Hon. Secretary:* Mr. J. R. Cummings, Thorverton, Devon. To give good sport throughout the river, a very wet season is wanted, for it soon runs down ;when, however, there is plenty of water, fish pass up into the Barle and the Somerset portion of the Exe.

The Chairman of the Board of Conservators is Mr. T. C. Daniel, Stuckeridge, Bampton. *Clerk:* Mr. Wm. H. Ford, Solicitor, Exeter.

The close times are for nets below Turf from ist September to ist March. Above Turf from ist September to 15th April. Rods from 2oth October to ist March.

6

SECTION 6

Chapter VI
THE TEIGN

The North and South Teign both rise in Dartmoor, to unite a little above Chagford Bridge, just below which the river passes through a narrow rocky gorge, and keeping an easterly direction, it flows under the bridges of Clifford and Dunsfbrd, where it turns to the south, and passing Chudleigh it is soon joined by the Bovey, the combined streams expanding into an estuary just below Newton Abbot, while five miles lower down it reaches the sea at Teignmouth, some five-and-thirty miles from its source, in which it drains 203 square miles. In 1862, owing to the poisons from a lead mine near Chudleigh opened some twenty years earlier, *salmonida* were practically wiped out. Prior to that the estuary used to be fished from March 4 to December 4 by eight boats, and the river itself was also profitably netted. In 1862 the mine ceased to work, and the water rising in the shaft, flowed in a constant stream into the river, while, as it held large quantities of copper, the fish were destroyed wholesale.

In 1863 an Angling Association was formed, and funds raised by annual subscription, but up to 1873 no salmon worth mentioning were caught by nets and none with rod. In 1873 and 1874 the Pollution Commission visited the river, and either enforced the law or persuaded the polluters to run their poisonous refuse into settling tanks. Their efforts were most successful, for in 1875 52 rod licences were issued at *Iqs. 6d.,* and though no returns are available as to the number of fish they caught, it is yet quite certain that such a large number of rods would not have taken out licences unless there had been good chances of sport.

1876. 41 licences at *los. 6d.* were issued.

1877. The netters took 22 salmon and 200 sea trout; 24 rod licences.

1878. 43 rod licencees took 8 salmon and 300 sea trout.

1879. Rod licence increased to *2os. ;* 27 licencees took 13 salmon averaging 7 Ibs. and 2,ooo migratory trout averaging 3lbs.

1880. Nets took 120 salmon ; 33 licencees took 10 salmon and 250 sea trout.

1881. 20 rod licencees took 7 salmon and 80 migratory trout.

I am somewhat doubtful if this is not an error of the 1879 Report of the Fishery Board, and that it should read 200, not 2,000.

1882. 24 rod licencees took 20 salmon averaging 8 Ibs., and 550 migratory trout weighing 750 Ibs.

1883. 28 rod licencees took 20 salmon and 700 migratory trout.

1884. Nets took 1,000 salmon, weighing 7,000 Ibs. ; 35 rods took 20 salmon and 300 migratory trout.

1885. 38 rods took 25 salmon and 120 migratory trout.

1886. 56 rod licences ; no record of their take.

1887. 55 rod licences: one of the worst seasons for some years.

1888. Nets took 700 salmon ; 77 rods took 1,000 migratory trout, weighing 800 Ibs.

1889. 72 rods took 50 salmon averaging 9 Ibs., and 860 migratory trout.

1890. Nets took 8,710 Ibs. ; 73 rods took 800 Ibs.

1891. Nets took 1,825 salmon ; 98 rods took 136 salmon and 400 migratory trout.

1892. Nets took 1,514 salmon ; 82 rods took 78 salmon and 502 migratory trout.

1893. Nets took 2,204 salmon, averaging 10 Ibs. ; 8r rods took 32 salmon and 1,000 migratory trout.

1894. Nets took 2,271 salmon; 87 rods took 45 salmon and 1,000 migratory trout.

1895. Nets took 2,547 salmon, averaging 10 Ibs.; 79rods took 23 salmon and 550 migratory trout. The best season on record for nets.

1896. Nets took 1,511 salmon; 65 rods took 30 salmon and 500 migratory trout.

1897. Nets took 1,329 salmon averaging 6 Ibs. ; 75 rods took 39 salmon and 500 migratory trout. In this year the Great Weeke Mine at Chagford was reopened, and pollutions were very bad.

1898. Nets took 483 salmon ; 48 rods took 19 salmon and 250 migratory trout.

1899. Nets took 876 salmon; 48 rods took 12 salmon and 300 migratory trout.

1900. Nets took 451 salmon ; 42 rods took 13 salmon and 300 migratory trout. March, April and May were very cold.

1901. Nets took 544 salmon ; 42 rods took 10 salmon and 200 migratory trout.

1902. Rods took 12 salmon averaging 9 Ibs., and 500 sea trout averaging i Ib.

The term " migratory trout" is used in the Reports of the Fishery Board, but the bulk of the take refers to sea trout or peel, probably mixed with a certain number of bull trout. In the five years following the reopening of the Great Weeke Mine with its attendant, but by no means necessary, pollutions, it will be seen how immediately the take of fishto nets and rods declined as a consequence of this poisoning. With regard to the Bovey tributary some six miles above its junction with the Teign, it is little more than a brook. Salmon are rarely caught in it, though grilse and sea trout are undoubtedly taken, now and again. There are two Angling Associations on the Teign ; the one for the Upper Teign, which extends from Chagford to Dunsford Bridge, is confined solely to trout, the salmon angling being reserved by the riparian owners.

Fish under five inches must be returned. No fishing allowed after 11 p.m. until 7 a.m. ; no wading except between Clifford and Steps Bridge ; no worm to be used below Sandy Park Bridge before ist June. Season tickets, *zis.* ; daily, *zs. 6d.* ; trout licence, *zs. 6d. Hon. Secretary:* Mr. C. G. Hayter-Hames, Chagford House.

Below this is the Lower Teign Association, extending from Steps Bridge down to the river mouth. Angling commences on March 3rd for salmon and trout, and for the latter ends 3Oth September, for the former 3131 October. Above Newbridge nothing but fly may be used until June ist, after that date any lawful bait may be worked, except between Bridford Weir and Bridford Bridge, where fly only may be used throughout the whole season, Below New Bridge fly and artificial minnow only until ist June, after which any

VOL. I.

- - –

lawful bait may be used. Wading is allowed above New Bridge all the season, but prohibited entirely below that point.

The use of the gaff is prohibited before ist May. No one may fish in Teign or Bovey with anything but trout flies unless he is the holder of a salmon licence.

Salmon licence, *2OS. ;* daily, *2s. ;* trout, *2S. 6d.* ; season ticket, 15. *6d.* for permanent residents within two miles of the river, to others *$2. is. od.* Weekly salmon tickets, 5$.; boys under 16 are charged half these rates. *Hon. Secretary;* Mr. H. G. Michelmore, Solicitor, Newton Abbot, who issues licences and tickets ; also Clarke, gunmaker, Newton Abbot ; Carpenter, " Globe " Hotel, Chudleigh ; Ladd, Post Office, Bovey Tracey, and Hill, Teignmouth. A comparison of the state of the Teign between 1860 and 1874, and that which has existed between 1875 and 1896, speaks eloquently of the very great benefits that the existing laws enable a good and resolute Board of Conservators to confer on any river.

From May to October is the best time for clean fish, while peel begin to run shortly before the salmon. The best flies are the Silver Doctor and other silver-bodied ones, Butcher, Childers, and Jock Scott, and the same for peel, only dressed on small hooks. As the water clears after a flood, the Devon and other artificial minnows are verydeadly. Annexed are the Rules of the Lower Teign Association.

RULES OF THE LOWER TEIGN FISHING ASSOCIATION
FOR 1903.

F. L. Carslake, Esq. Gen. Mackay Heriot. Lieut.-Col. F. Trimmer.
T. W. Donaldson, Esq. F. W. Marshal, Esq. Mr. J. B. Truman.
P. G. Dobson, Esq. H. A. Price, Esq.

i.|That the object of this Association is to carry out the provisions of the Salmon and Fresh Water Fishery Acts and to protect such parts of the River Teign and its tributaries, from Steps Bridge to the mouth (with the exception of the River Lemon) as may be granted by the Proprietors to be preserved by it.

2.|Landowners who give up their rights to the Association and holders of non-transferable season tickets who have taken out yearly salmon licences for the previous year, and reside within two miles of the River Teign or Bovey, shall be Members of the Association.

N.B.|It shall be the duty of the Secretary to present to the Annual General Meeting in each year a list of such season ticket- holders, and that list shall remain in force till the next Annual General Meeting.

Za.|Landowners, Members of the Association, shall at the discretion of the Committee have two tickets free of cost, one to be transferable, and all tenants renting lands bordering on the river, whose landlords are Members of the Association, shall be entitled to one non-transferable ticket which may be transferred to any member of his family at the discretion of the Secretary.

3.|That no person be allowed to fish without a ticket, which must be shown to the Keeper or any Member of the Association, when demanded.

N.B.|No fishing, either for salmon or trout, allowed without a licence from the Board of Conservators as well as the AssociationTicket. The price of licences is at present fixed at i for a season licence for salmon ; 2s. for daily licences ; and 25. dd. for season licence for trout.

4. | The price of a season ticket is 15. 6d. for persons permanently residing within two miles of the Rivers Teign or Bovey, for others the price of a season ticket is $2. 25. The price of the weekly ticket is 51., and monthly ticket ios., both irrespective of residence. Boys under 16 at half the above rates. Members of the Association shall be entitled to daily tickets for any friends staying with them, or who accompany them when fishing. The price of such tickets shall be 2S. per day, and they are only obtainable direct from the Hon. Secretary.

N.B. | For the purpose of the above rule present Members of the Association residing without the two miles limit shall be considered as residing within the limit.

5. | No fishing except with rod and line is permitted, all fish of less than seven inches in length must be returned to the water, and every person fishing shall put all the fish he retains into a bag or basket, which shall always be open, on demand, to the inspection of the Water Bailiff.

N.B. | The use of the gaff is prohibited before the ist May. Fishing shall commence on the 3rd day of March, and end for trout on the 3Oth day of September, and for salmon on the 3151 day of October. No fishing of any kind is permitted on Sundays.

7. | In the river Teign above Newbridge nothing but artificial fly shall be used until the ist June, but on and after that day any lawful bait may be used, except between Bridford Weir and Bridford Bridge, where only artificial fly shall be used throughout the season. Below New Bridge artificial minnow and artificial fly only are allowed until the ist June, after which date any lawful bait may be used. Wading is allowed above New Bridge throughout the season, but below that point it is prohibited.

8. I In the river Bovey wading is at all times prohibited and only artificial fly (without gentles attached) is allowed until the ist June, on and after which day artificial minnow may be used.

9.INo one may fish in either Teign or Bovey, except with artificial fly for trout only, unless he be the holder of a salmon licence from the Teign Board of Conservators.

10.INo dogs shall be allowed to accompany persons whilst fishing, and all persons *shall* shut the gates and trespass as little as possible. No Member of the Association shall, on any account, cut or injure any of the bushes on the banks of the river without the permission of the Tenant. Trespassing on mowing grass is especially prohibited, and anyone infringing this rule will be held personally liable for all damage done by him.

ii.IThat no Keeper in the pay of the Association be allowed to fish.

12.IThe Annual General Meeting of the Association shall be held on the first Thursday in February, when the Hon. Treasurer and Secretary, and a Committee of eight shall be appointed, who shall have power to add to their number. The Hon. Secretary shall be an additional member of the Committee. The affairs of the Association shall be managed by the Committee, who shall meet at least once every year, and all questions arising under the Rules, or the construction of them, shall be decided by them without appeal, but no new rule shall be made or existing rule altered, in whole or part, except at the Annual General Meeting in February, nor then, unless notice of the intention to propose such new rule or alteration, or rescission of existing rule has been given to the Secretary, seven days at least before the date of the Annual General Meeting. It shall be the duty of the Secretary to send notice of such intended proposition to all members of the Association.

13.IAny person holding a ticket and not complying with the Rules of the Association, or committing any breach of the Salmon Fishery Acts, or so conducting himself as to be an annoyance to other people on the river, shall forfeit his ticket, and shall be suspended from fishing again at the discretion of the Committee.

Harold G. Michelmore, *Hon. Secrttaty.*

Tickets and Licences may be obtained from Messrs. Hacker, Michelmore & Bewes, Solicitors, Newton Abbot, and Chudleigh; from Mr. Clarke,

VOL. I. E

fishing-tackle dealer, Newton Abbot; Mr. Carpenter, " Globe " Hotel, Chudleigh ; Mrs. Hellier, " Dolphin" Hotel; Mr. Beer, Railway Hotel; Mr. Ladd, Post Office, Bovey Tracey; and Mr. Hill, Teignmouth; or from the Hon. Secretary.

N.B.ISeason salmon licences can only be obtained from the Clerks to the Conservators, Messrs. Hacker, Michelmore & Bewes. Tickets for residents within the two mile limit, and monthly and weekly tickets, can be obtained from any distributor. Tickets for persons entitled thereto under the N.B. to Rule 4, end all other tickets, can only be obtained on application by letter to the Hon. Secretary, Mr. Harold G. Michelmore, Devonia, Newton Abbot.

LOWER TEIGN FISHING ASSOCIATION.

The Water Reserved by the above Association is as follows:

River Teign.

Commencing from the Kingsteignton Road, the water on the left bank is reserved by the Owners as far as Fishwick, but on the right bank the first field above the Kingsteignton Road, and the first field below Teign- bridge, is given to the Association, From Teighbridge to Fishwick the water is reserved on both banks by the Owner. From Fishwick the River belongs to the Association up to, but not including, the field which contains Gooseham Footbridge, that field and Lower Gooseham are reserved by the Owner, but the right bank of Higher Gooseham is given to the Association, as also is Bawdon's Marsh at the junction of the Bovey.

From here, with the exception of one field on the left bank looking up stream opposite Chudleigh Railway Station, the water is given to, or rented by the Association, the whole way to Canonteign (between Trusham and Ashton), with the exception of Northwood Farm, which lies between Putts Hill and Farley Mill, (i.e., just below Trusham), on the right bank going up, and with the exception of Lady Exmouth's water which lies between Doghole Plantation and Canonteign on the left bank going up.Mr. Treeby's water (both banks), which stretches from the notice board at the bottom of the meadow below the old mine at Canonteign to the top of Ashton Weir pool, is reserved by the Owner. The Association then own the water up to, but not including the first field below Teign House. The land adjoining the new railway is given to the Association, but Mr. Byrom's two fields below Bridford Bridge are reserved by the Owner. The water belongs to the Association on the right bank looking up stream from Bridford Bridge to Bridford Weir. Members of the Association are not entitled during the present season to fish above Bridford Weir.

River Bovey.

The River Bovey from its junction with the Teign up to Jewsbridge is preserved by the Owner. From Jewsbridge upwards for about a mile it is preserved by the Association, with the exception of the small copse on the right bank just above Jewsbridge, belonging to Mr. St. Maur, and on the left bank the first field above and the first field below where the railway crosses the stream, which belongs to Mr. J. Wright The water immediately below Bovey Tracey belonging on the right bank to Miss Divett, and on the left bank to Mrs. Bentinck, is not given to the Association.

N.B.|The right and left banks are referred to looking up stream.

H. G. Michelmore, *Hon. Sec. February,* 1903.

On the lower part of the river Mr. H. S. Maur, of Hever, Newton Abbot, has some nice water on the Teign and Lower Bovey, part of which is let on lease, while he keeps the remainder in his own hands. Wading is not advisable, as the lower reaches are deep, but there are some twenty good catches between Bridford Weir and the estuary,which can all be cast from the bank: The Signal Posts, Chudleigh Weir Pool, New Bridge Pool, Bawdon's, Bovey Junction, Clam Pool, Over the Way, Preston Flat, and Forlorn Hope, are some of the best. Silver Doctor, Wilkinson, Butcher, Lion, Black Doctor, are the favourites, medium size. The Devon Minnow and Brown's Phantom also kill well, but can only be used subject to the restrictions printed in the Rules of the Association. Each rod generally gets about 10 fish a season ; in 1891 250 were caught.

There is a run of " peal" (as sea trout are called here) in the spring, some bull trout coming with them, the former weighing from 2 to 5 Ibs. In July and August there is a further run of harvest peall*i.e.,* sea trout grilse, or herling, as they are called in Scotland. Small, silver-bodied flies, Wasp, Blue and Silver, Red Palmer, Grey Moth, Alexandra, with Jungle Cock Cheeks, are the best. The Teign runs very low in dry summers. Mr. F. W. Marshall, of Oakley, Newton Abbot, who rents the lowest mile-and-a-half of the Bovey, tells me that the estuary is now fished by some fifteen boats with a .$5 licence ; that they all do fairly well, one boat in 1902 taking 17 salmon in a single haul. In another year a fish of 42 Ibs. was caught in the nets at Teignmouth, while Mr. Marshall landed a kelt of 35 Ibs. inthe spring of 1902. In his opinion, the stake nets along the coasts between Babbacombe and Teignmouth do a great deal of harm to the Teign, as they intercept nearly all the fish that would otherwise come up the river. Mr. H. A. Price, of Newton Abbot, who has fished the river for the past twenty-five years, tells me that he has never killed more than 2 clean salmon in a day, but that in the past he has killed 9 sea trout in a day with the fly, although even they are not nearly so numerous as they were. The Board of Conservators is, however, a strong one, and the anglers of the district are very hopeful of an improvement.

The *Chairman of the Board* is Lord Clifford, Ugbrooke Park, Chudleigh. *Clerks:* Messrs. Hacker and Michelmore, Newton Abbot.

The close time for nets is from August 3151 to 2nd March; for rods from 3131 October to 2nd March.

7

SECTION 7

Chapter VII
THE DART

Has a course of about 30 miles with a catchment basin of 200 square miles; it is formed by the junction of several small streams running off Dartmoor and does not assume any noticeable proportions before reaching Dart Meet Bridge, where the river proper is joined by the West Dart, below which it passes Holne Park to reach Buckfastleigh, and then with a further run of about eight miles it falls over Totnes Weir to expand into a long narrow estuary. From Dart Meet, which is 800 feet above sea level, the river runs with great swiftness. In 1862 it was so prolific that many of the natives of Buckfastleigh did nothing but fish; they sold and they ate their takes, which they made in defiance of the close time, and clean and unclean fish with fry in thousands were taken by these men. It is a fairly early river, and, though the main harvest is in August, clean run salmon are taken as early as March.

A Board of Conservators was formed in 1866, issuing rod licences at 20. each.

1868. 41 rod licences.

1869. 46 rod licences.

1870. About 7,000 fish netted; 32 rod licencees, who took only 15 salmon, on account of a very dry season.

1871. 41 licences; no returns of rods or nets.

1872. 44 licences.

1&73- 45 licences.

1874. 34 licences; Totnes Weir, which belonged to the Duke of Cleveland, formed a great obstruction to the passage of the salmon. Pollutions from manufactories were also very bad.

1&75- 39 licences; about 50 salmon of 20 Ibs. were netted in the autumn and passed over Totnes Weir.

1876. 41 licences.

1877. 41 licences; about 7,400 fish netted of 10 Ibs. average weight, the rods caught next to none, on account of the obstruction at Totnes Weir.

1878. 34 licences; in this season, which was a very wet one, salmon and migratory tout pushed their way up to the very sources of the river, and were seen close to Dartmoor Prison.

These migratory trout were variously described as grilse, sea trout, harvest peal, bull trout, and " truff." The Fishery Board Report of 1879 describes the Harvest Cock or Harvest Peal as an autumn fish which runs up the smallrivers of Devon, probably analagous to the " Whitlaws " of Scotland, the "Lammas Trout" of the Tay, "Trout Peal" of Ireland, and Sewin of Wales. In the Dart they run from 3 to 6 Ibs. In about 1820, salmon, or else sea trout of from 10 to 12 Ibs. in weight, used to run up the Thames in harvest time. The truff is described as probably the grilse of the bull trout or a variety of the bull trout. 1%79- 37 rd licences.

1880. 29 rod licences. Fish weighing up to 30 Ibs. were passed over Totnes Weir, which changed hands this year, when arrangements were at once made by the Conservators for the construction of a fish pass.

1881. 36 rod licencees, who took 60 fish of from 4 to 16 Ibs. As the fish pass in Totnes Weir was not finished, 117 salmon were netted below and turned in above it.

1882. About 3,743 fish netted. The rods caught 82 fish, and 80 others were lifted over the still unfinished weir.

1883. 56 rod licencees, who got 60 fish. The fish pass in Totnes Weir was finished and worked well.

1884. 45 licences ; a very dry season and poor sport.

1885. 45 licencees took 80 fish, averaging 10 Ibs. each.

1886. 68 licencees took about 100 fish.

1887. It was estimated that the seventeen boats working the estuary took about 8,000 fish ; it would require at leastthat number for each boat to make a profit, and they all made large ones. 57 rod licencees caught under a dozen fish, owing to a very dry season.

1888. 63 rod licencees caught 158 fish. A good fish pass was erected at Buck-fastleigh.

1889. 71 rod licencees caught 60 fish,

1890. 75 ,, 100

1891. 93 ,, about 300 fish.

1892. 93 250

1893. 100 100

1894. 133 274 of ii to 12 Ibs. average weight. A great flood destroyed Totnes Weir.

1895. 67 licences at 20. ; 43 at 75. 6d. a month ; they caught 163 fish of from 8 to 15 Ibs. in weight.

1896. 92 licencees caught 156 fish.

1897. 90 138 ; a very dry season.

1898. 68 ,, ,, 95 ,, ; another very dry season.

1899. The nets were estimated to have caught 1,700 fish averaging 10 Ibs. ; 73 licencees caught 67 fish of 12 Ibs. average weight; again a very dry season.

1900. Nets caught 1,282 fish; 75 licencees caught 115 of 10 Ibs. average weight.

1901. Nets caught 1,902 fish ; 65 licencees took 90 fish,of which only about a dozen were killed on the Association's water. Season licences are 2O.y. ; weekly ones, 75. 6d. ; daily ones, 45.

1902. Nets caught 1,728 salmon; rods caught 158 salmon, weighing 1,805 Ibs. 74 rod licences at 2O.r. ; 52 ditto weekly, 75. 6d. ; 5 ditto day, 5$.

Though it is chiefly on those private waters which are some ten miles above Totnes that the bulk of the rod take is made, the Dart Angling Association has a stretch of seven miles immediately above Totnes Weir; owing, however, to the excellent fish passes the fish travel through this reach very quickly, but yet there are always a certain number of salmon and truff captured in it.

The Rules of the Association are as under :|

THE DART ANGLING ASSOCIATION.

Season, 1902.

President: Arthur M. Champernowne, Esq.

Vice-President: John Fleming, Esq. *Honorary Secretary:* Mr. George F. Kellock, Solicitor, Totnes.

The waters over which the Association Tickets are available consist of:|

The left bank of the River Dart from Austin's Bridge, Buckfastleigh, to the mouth of the Hems, below Totnes Weir;

The right bank of the River from the Railway Bridge, below Austin's Bridge, down to Hood Bridge;

Both banks of the Hems from By Cellars, above Littlehempstone, to the junction of the River with the Dart.

The Prices of Tickets are;

$ J. d. i.|Whole Season for Salmon and Trout ... i o o

2.|Weekly ...076

3.|Daily ...026

4.|Whole Season for Trout only ... ... o 10 o

5.|Monthly from ist May 050

6.|Daily 020

N.B.|Holders of Association Fishing Tickets are not exempt from the

necessity of procuring a Licence from the Dart Board of Conservators
before commencing to fish.

Regulations For Fishing.

i.|Nursery Pool is specially reserved for fly fishing only; no bait of any description,
except artificial flies, may be used between the Notice Board at the head of the Pool
and the Railway Bridge below it.

2.|Holders of Salmon Tickets only shall be allowed to fish between the head of
Totnes Weir and the Railway Bridge below the Weir, after 9 o'clock at night, from the
ist June to the end of the season.

3.|No fish is to be retained under 7 inches (measured from nose to fork of tail). All
fish are to be carried in baskets or bags, which must be exhibited to the Keepers, or
any Member of the Committee on demand, under a penalty of 5. for each offence.

4.|No worm fishing is allowed in any part of the River before ist April or before ist
May above Hood Bridge.

5.|No hook to be used with any minnow larger than No. 3.

6.|No lead may be used nearer than 8 inches to the hook.

7.|Fishing is not allowed on Sundays.

8.|Anglers must confine themselves to the path by the margin of the River.

On no account must they step into any standing crops or

mowing grass. No dog is allowed with an Angler or with anyfriend who may
accompany him under a penalty of y. for each

offence.

9.|If the Committee are satisfied that any Member or Ticket-holder has left a gate
unfastened after having passed through it, he shall pay the sum of 5. to the Secretary
on his demand, and will be liable in addition for any injury caused by stock straying
or trespassing, or any other damage.

The netting of the pool below Totnes Weir, which belongs to the Duchess of
Cleveland, is rented by a club of gentlemen so that it may not pass into the hands of
professional netters, who would work it to make every penny they could. This club
makes a certain amount of profit, which they spend on improving the river, or on local
charities; during the last few years they have disbursed some hundreds of pounds in
improving the fish passes, and putting on extra water bailiffs in the spawning season,
and it would be well for all rivers if this excellent example were more often followed.
The standard patterns of flies will kill, medium size to quite small, the silver-bodied
ones are the favourites ; a rod of from 14 to 16 ft. will be ample.

The *Chairman of the Board of Conservators* is The Hon. Robert Dawson, Holne
Park. *Clerk:* Mr. E. Windeatt, Totnes.

Close times for nets from iyth August to 28th February; for rods from ist October
to 28th February.

8

SECTION 8

Chapter VIII
THE AVON AND ERME

The Avon rises on the southern borders of Dartmoor, adjacent to the sources of the Erme, the Yealm, and the Plym. With a total length of about twenty-five miles and a drainage area of fifty-four square miles, it flows nearly due south past Brent, Moreleigh and Loddiswell, to fall at Aveton Gifford into a long narrow estuary.

GARRA BRIDGE. BELOW LODDISWELL.

VOL. I.

The Erme, with a course of about fifteen miles and a drainage area of forty-three square miles, passes Ivy bridge, to fall also into a narrow estuary some three miles below Ermington; it is chiefly a river for sea trout, which begin to appear in March, and continue to run during April, May, and part of June. The first comers vary in weight from i to 4 Ibs., and these are followed by the " school peel," which are the grilse of sea trout|" finnocks," as they are called in Scotland|which continue to run until about the middle of August.

In 1860 the Avon was infested with poachers, chiefly spearers; no one interfered with [them ; while at Aveton Gifford there was a mill and fishery weir, which was so nearly insurmountable that proceedings were taken against the owner to compel him to place a fish pass in it. In 1866 a Board of Conservators was formed, in which the Erme proprietors did not join. This Board was in addition to a local Angling Association already formed, and, combining together, they attacked the poaching evil with such vigour that prosecutions and convictions were so plentiful that at length the wrongdoers desisted, when they found they could no longer carry on the industry with impunity. In 1867 there were 15 rod licences issued at *zos.* Poaching was still prevalent in the upper waters, where there were many small proprietors who took no interest in salmonpreservation, while the funds at the disposal of the Conservators were not sufficient to protect the whole river. A few clean fish appeared in February and March, but the main harvest was in July and August, followed by a heavy run in October and November.

1868. Nets took 140 salmon. First clean fish taken end of May, but some " truff" were got in February and March ; 14 rod licencees took 30 salmon.

1869. 18 rod licencees took 75 salmon.

1870. 20 rod licencees took between 70 and 80 salmon.

1870. On the Erme the paper mill at Ivybridge turned so much pollution into the river as to cause it in dry weather to smell like a sewer.

1871. There was some trouble between the Conservators and Proprietors as to the use by anglers of their respective banks ; kelts were openly sold at Aveton Gifford at *d.* a pound; 23 rod licencees took between 40 and 50 salmon.

1872. 17 rod licences issued. No record of catch, but it is stated that both nets and rods kept all kelts; and it was proposed that the river should not be opened until ist April.

1873. Open time altered from February 2 to September i, and decreed to be from April i to 21 September; 33 rod licences issued. They kiUed very few clean fish, but took about 100 kelts, and the nets many more!

1874. The Erme fish were reported as nearly wiped out by the Ivy bridge pollutions.

1875. 2O rd licences issued ; no record.

1876. 9 rod licences issued; they refused to give any information of their takes.

1877. 16 rod licences ; no record.

1877. In the Erme 6 salmon averaging 8 Ibs., and 1,200 sea trout of about 3 Ibs., were caught by nets.

1878. Nets took in the Erme 3 or 4 salmon and 1,053 migratory trout, averaging 2 Ibs.

1879. Nets took about 700 sea trout in the Erme.

1880. The Erme nets took 3 salmon and 800 trout, averaging 2 Ibs. On the Avon a fish of 47- Ibs. was netted at Bantham ; 17 rod licences issued.

1881. 21 rod licences; about 100 fish, weighing 1,200 Ibs., caught by rod in Avon, On the Erme, nets took 4 salmon and 1,298 migratory trout, averaging 2 Ibs.

1882. 22 rod licences. On Avon, rods took about 100 fish of 12 Ibs. each ; there was a first appearance of disease. On the Erme the nets took 30 salmon and 1,414 migratory trout.

1883. 31 rod licences ; 154 salmon caught in Avon, The Erme nets took 9 salmon and 1,702 migratory trout; disease bad in both rivers.

1884. 27 rod licences. Anglers caught in Avon no salmon weighing 1,320 Ibs. and 100 migratory trout of i Ib. each. The Erme nets took 964 migratory trout.

1885. 25 rod licences. Anglers in Avon took 81 salmon. Erme nets took i salmon and 261 migratory trout. In this year the netting season was prolonged until 3ist October, when many fish of 20 to 30 Ibs. each were caught " in splendid condition " according to the fishermen. *Credat Judesus !* For I doubt if any salmon caught at the end of October can really be properly described as in prime condition. The netters, as usual, refused any information as to their takes.

1886. 27 rod licences. Anglers caught in Avon 152 salmon weighing 1,824 Ibs. and 100 migratory trout of I Ib. The Erme nets took 1,148 migratory trout.

1887. 12 rod licences. No records of either river.

1888. The many complaints made by the London Fish Salesmen of the bad condition of salmon sent for sale in October led to alterations of the close time, and it was ordered to be from 3Oth September to ist May in lieu of November ist to 4th April. 24 rod licences. No report. The Erme nets took i salmon and 745 migratory trout.

1889. 24 rod licences. No records.

1890. 8 rod licences. Anglers on Avon took 3 salmon and 25 migratory trout. The Erme nets took 1,193 migratory trout.

VOL. I.

1891. 10 rod licences. No record of either river.

1892. 14 ,, ,, ,, ,,

1%93- 19 .

1894 22

A large number of spawning fish " snatched" on the upper waters.

1895. 16 rod licences. No record of either river.

1896. 12 ,, ,, ,,

I&97- I5 .   "

1898. 20 ,.

!899- 9 ,, ,. .. .. .

1900. 13

1901- 9

1902. o ,, ,, ,, ,, ,, ,,

From the above records it will be seen that from 1868 to 1889 the fish responded freely to the efforts made for their preservation, and that from 1880 to 1889 there was an average of 23 rod licences for the ten years, while the twelve following years, from 1890 to 1901, only show an average of 14 licences. It is also remarkable that, while the Erme gives no statistics as to the take of migratory trout by the rod, but full ones so far as the netting is concerned, the Avon reverses the position and, withholding all netting returns, it gives in most years full details of the rod captures. The present close times on thez o

S Cd *in* o z

X

H

Avon are for nets from 3Oth September to ist May, for rods from 3Oth November to ist May. On the Erme the close time for nets is from 3Oth September to 4th April, and for rods from 3oth November to 4th April.

From Brent to Gara the Avon is for the most part rocky and narrow and a good deal of it is in private hands, though the farmers are very liberal in giving permission. It is hard fished by the residents of Brent and is by no means the best four miles of the river, although occasionally good fish are taken in it; the best of it is from Bickham Bridge to Gara. From Gara to Loddiswell The Avon Fishing Association has both banks continuously for between four and five miles, which is the best part of the river, especially above Topsham Bridge. Below Loddiswell Weir the angling down to Hack Bridge is in private hands. Below this the Association again comes in and extends to within two fields of Aveton Gifford Weir, in which portion wading is prohibited ; but on these lower reaches a good westerly breeze is desirable, as the water is rather dead.

AVON FISHING ASSOCIATION.

Rules.

i.|This Association is called the Avon Fishing Association, and is formed to improve the fishing in the river Avon, and to assist the Board of Conservators of the district.

2.|All persons who grant fishing rights to the Association are Honorary Members of the Association, and are entitled, in the case of grantors of fishing rights extending a quarter of a mile and upwards, to Two Free Transferable Season Fishing Tickets, and in the case of grantors of fishing rights extending less than a quarter of a mile, to one Free Transferable Season Fishing Ticket.

3.|All occupiers of land with a water frontage of a quarter of a mile and upwards, the fishing rights over which have been granted to the Association, are Honorary Members of the Association, and are entitled to One Free Transferable Season Fishing Ticket, but notwithstanding anything contained in this or the preceding rule, the Committee of the Association may in special cases make other arrangements with owners of fishing rights.

4.|The Transferable Tickets mentioned in Rules 2 and 3 may be used by the grantor or occupier himself, a resident member of his family, or a guest or lodger staying in his house, except that a lodger may only use a Free Transferable Ticket for two consecutive weeks in one season, and thereafter shall not be entitled to fish without payment.

5.|The only Fishing Tickets issued are Season Tickets at $2, Monthly Tickets at $i, and Weekly Tickets at 105. All holders of Season Tickets, who are of full age, will be enrolled as Members of the Association. The period of membership of the Association shall be for one year, calculated from the ist February in each year. Not more than 30 season fishing tickets (other than transferable tickets) shall be issued in any one season, and not more than two monthly tickets nor more than five weekly tickets shall be running at the same time.

6.|No bait for trout, except artificial fly, may be used until after the 3ist May, when worm or minnow may be used. No worm fishing is allowed at any time between Gara Bridge and Bickham Railway Bridge (see notice board). *No salmon fishing with minnow is allowed after the 1st October. No lead may be used nearer than 8 inches to the hook.*

7.|No fish may be retained under 7 inches in length (measured from nose to fork of tail), except in the Glazebrook Stream and above Shipley Bridge.

8.|Fishing is not allowed on Sunday, or during the night, viz.: | from an hour after sunset until an hour before sunrise, except during June and July, when it may be prosecuted until 10 p.m.

9.|No Member or Ticket-holder of the Association is allowed to sell his fish or otherwise dispose of them for profit.

10.|Fishing Tickets and Licences must be exhibited by Anglers to any Member of the Association on production of his Ticket, and also to the Keepers, on being required.

ii.|Anglers must confine themselves to the path by the margin of the river. On no account must they step into any standing crop or mowing grass.

12.|No dogs are allowed with an angler or with any friend who may accompany him.

13.|If the Committee are satisfied that any Ticket-holder has left a gate unfastened after having passed through it, he shall pay the sum of 5. to the Secretary on his demand, and will be liable in addition for any damage caused by stock straying or trespassing, or any other damage.

14.|No wading is allowed below Loddiswell Bridge.

15.|The Annual General Meeting of the Association shall be held in the second week in January at South Brent, when a Committee shall be elected and a Secretary appointed for managing the affairs of the Association. Any three Members of the Committee may instruct the Secretary to call a Special General Meeting of the Association at any time. Seven days' notice shall be given of any such Meeting, and no other business than that stated in the notice shall be discussed at that Meeting. Seven Members shall form a quorum at a General Meeting.

16.|The Committee shall meet quarterly at South Brent and Kings- bridge alternately. The Secretary may call a Meeting of the Committee at any time; three Members shall form a quorum at a Committee Meeting.

17.|These rules may be altered from time to time by a majority of three-fifths of the Members present at a General Meeting of the Association. Notice of any such proposed alteration must be given by the Secretary to each Member seven days before the meeting.

18.|The surplus funds of the Association, after providing for rents, expenses, and a reasonable working balance, shall be handed over to the Board of Conservators for the Avon district, to be used by them in such manner as they may deem most expedient for the protection and improvement of the fishing in the district.

19.|Any complaints of unfair fishing, unsportsmanlike conduct, or any other matter, must be sent to the Secretary, who shall, if necessary, call a Special Meeting of the Committee to consider such communication.

20.lThe Committee may, in their absolute discretion, cancel any ticket if they are satisfied that the holder has contravened any rules of the Association or any provision of the Salmon and Freshwater Fisheries Acts.

21.lA copy of the Rules shall be issued with each ticket, receipt of which will be considered as an agreement by the Ticket-holder to be bound
thereby.

C. E. Turner, Solicitor, Salcombe,
Dated zyd January, 1903. *Secretary.*

N.B.lHolders of Association Fishing Tickets are not exempt from the necessity of procuring a licence from the Avon and Erme Board of Conservators before commencing to fish.

Conservators' Licences can be obtained from the Secretary. The prices are:lSalmon (including Trout), Season only, *$i*; Trout, Season, *los.;* Trout, weekly, 5$.; Trout, day, *2s.*

At the present day the whole water is better for trout than for salmon, though both have woefully decreased, and a lo-lb. basket is very rare, though formerly it was quite common. Some of the trout run as heavy as 2 Ibs., but not many, and those of that weight usually fall victims to minnow or worm. The natives have ceased to regard the Avon as a salmon river, for they look upon it as being used entirelyas a spawning ground, and fish do not enter in any numbers till late in October. Wading stockings suffice, and the cream of the trout season is from middle of April to end of June. In March and April the best flies are Blue Dun, Blue Upright, Half Stone, March Brown, Cowdung, and Cochy- bonddhu. May and June, Black Hawthorn, Blue Dun, Alder, Welshman's Button. July and August, Alder, Black Gnat, Willow, Soldier, and August Dun. It is by no means an easy river to fish when the water is low and bright.

The Avon Association tickets are *$2* for the season, *$i* for a month, and *los.* for a week, and season tickets are limited to thirty. Up till 3151 May artificial fly only is allowed; after that date minnow and worm may be used No salmon fishing with minnow allowed after ist October.

For trout the limit length is 7 inches. No Sunday or night fishing from an hour after sunset to an hour before sunrise, but in June and July it may be continued up till 10 p.m. No ticket-holder to sell his fish. Salmon licences, which include trout, *2is.* Trout only, for season, *ios.,* weekly, *55.,* day, *zs.* The few salmon that are now caught in the river are usually taken with Devon minnows, but the small standard patterns of flies sometimes kill. The Secretary of the Association is Mr. C. E. Turner, Solicitor, Salcombe.

With regard to the Erme, it was also preserved by the Angling Association until the end of 1902, when, as the expense of putting on a watcher was by no means in accord with the results obtained, the preservation was given up.

The *Chairman of the Board of Conservators* is Mr. F. S. Cornish Bowden, Black Hall, South Brent. *Clerk,* Mr. W. Beer, Kingsbridge.

9

SECTION 9

Chapter IX
  THE PLYM, TAVY, TAMAR, WALKHAM,
YEALM, AND LYNHER.

As these rivers are all in one Fishery District, it will be as well to deal with them in the order in which they come from East to West. Commencing, then, with the Yealm, which rises in the south of Dartmoor, and after a fairly straight run of some twelve miles, falls into a long estuary
  THE YEALM ESTUARY.
at Yealmpton, eventually to join the sea in Wembury Bay, it is sad to relate that, owing to the pollutions from mines, the sea troutlit was never . much of a salmon streamlhave been almost wiped out, though formerly they abounded, and as late as 1879 one estuary net took 3 salmon and 400 sea trout in the season, while prior to that larger takes were made.
  Passing on then to the Plym, which rises in Erme Head, one of the Dartmoor hills, and after a run of about eight miles is joined by the Meavy at Shaugh Bridge, from which junction it has a further run of eight miles before falling into Plymouth Sound, to the east of the townlthe Plym proper is formed by the junction of the Plym

(or Cad as it is more often called by the natives) and the Meavy at Shaugh Bridge, two miles from Bickleigh Station on the Launceston Branch of the Great Western Railway. Below the junction the river is entirely in private hands, but from Shaugh Bridge upwards for some nine miles, it is in the hands of the Tavy, Walkham and Plym Fishing Association. Up to Cadover Bridge it flows through a rocky, precipitous gorge, which can only be fished by able-bodied active anglers, who are accustomed to clambering. There are many good pools in this reach which hold salmon, sea trout, and brown trout in fair numbers, but, nevertheless, the angler who is " no verra sureof himself" had better pass this bit of fishing and take the road to Shaugh Prior before commencing operations, for once above Cadover Bridge he will find himself in moorland, with six miles of good angling above him. The brownies are small, as is the case with all the streams of Dartmoor, though occasionally a heavy one may be got. Four miles above Cadover Bridge is Didsbury Warren, where the river narrows very much and forms a succession of falls locally known as Plym Steps. Above this trout rise freely in a spate, and seven or eight dozen may at times be taken by anyone who is on the spot at the right moment; which is but of short duration, as the river falls with great rapidity. The same flies that kill on the Walkham may safely be used here, only they should be rather smaller. May and June are the best months for trout, August and September for sea trout.

The Meavy, for more than a mile above the junction at Shaugh Bridge, is strewn with boulders of all sizes and shapes, while the flow of the river is very rapid. A mile-and-a-half up stream Goodameavy Bridge is reached, and here there are some decent trout, while after June sea trout find their way to the deeper pools : much of the water hereabouts is overhung, and fly-fishing is difficult and makes wading a necessity. A mile further up is Hoomeavey Bridge, with a good pool just below it, which always holds some large brownies, and isalso a pretty sure find after June for a few sea trout, while in the autumn it is a good cast for a salmon. From this point up to Meavy village the river widens considerably, and there are fine reaches of gravel interspersed with pools which are the favourite spawning grounds of the salmon. There is a comfortable inn in the village with a remarkably large and ancient oak tree opposite to it. Above Meavy Bridge, up to the Reservoir which supplies Plymouth with water, there is some good trouting, but the Reservoir itself is in private hands and fished by the landowners in conjunction with the Waterworks Company. It is well stocked with fine trout, some of which run up to 6 lbs. Above the Reservoir the Association again comes in, and the stream divides itself, each of them containing numerous small trout. The sea trout of the Plym run somewhat earlier than in the neighbouring streams; they are taken as early as March, and gradually increase in numbers to the middle of June ; in 1878 as many as 900 were netted in one day, of which 200 were got at one haul.

The river suffers considerably from the pollution of lead mines and the milky discharge from china clay works.

We now come to the Tavy, which enjoys the reputation of being the best salmon and sea trout river of South Devon. It rises from Cranmere Pool on Dartmoor, and has a run of about

seventeen miles before it forms an estuary a little below Buck- land Abbey, while Tavistock is the principal town on its banks. Some three miles above Saltash, its estuary joins that of the Tamar, to find its waters reaching the sea in Plymouth Sound. The brownies of its head waters are small, and hardly weigh five to the pound. Salmon or sea trout (peal or peel) enter some time about the end of April, though the main run does not come till the end of May or early in June. These early salmon weigh about 10 Ibs. and sea trout 2 Ibs. In July grilse and the "school peel," or finnocks, begin to run, and continue to do so till the end of the season. The latter average a bare $ lb., and with them come the salmon, though they are not in great numbers, and two dozen will perhaps fully represent the average rod take of each year. From Tavistock down to the " Double Waters " at Walkham Junction, the river is owned by the Duke of Bedford ; this stretch is about six miles in length, and the Duke's agent issues tickets to the working men of Tavistock at *is.* each, though in addition they have to take out a salmon rod licence at 12*s. 6d.*; at one time sport was so good that they could easily recoup themselves for this outlay by selling their fish, while some of them are said to have made quite a nice little profit. From the " Double Waters " the Association has the angling on the left bank down to the Lady Bertha Mine,

VOL. J.

where Sir Massey Lopes and Lord Seaton keep their fishings in their own hands. On the right bank the Association has the fishing to the end of Tames Weir pool, about a quarter- of-a-mile above Denham Bridge. Then, on the right bank, Lord Mount Edgecumbe reserves his rights to the tidal water ; but if he is not in residence an application for a day to the Manor House, Stonehouse, will, as a rule, be favourably entertained. The best months are July and August, when most of the peel are taken between 9 and 10 o'clock p.m. ; the river, however, is uncertain, and many days which appear perfect result only in an empty basket. Devon Minnows and Phantoms account for the bulk of the fish that are caught in the daytime, while small silver and black and blue Doctors, Jock Scotts, Aylmers, Cochybonddhus, Red Palmers, and Alders are successful, and where the river is big large sizes of these flies do well. The river rises and falls very quickly, and to ensure success the angler must be on the spot.

In 1878 there were 1,500 sea trout caught by anglers in the Tavy and Walkham,

In 1879 52 rods had a few salmon and 1,116 sea trout.

The Walkham also rises on Dartmoor some three miles to the north-east of Prince Town. From its source down to Huckworthy Bridge it is very rocky and much overhung, until three miles lower down it reaches Merivale Bridge. Amile-and-a-half below is Horrabridge, a fair sized village with two inns, and from thence to Grenofen Bridge there are a series of nice-looking pools which hold peal in July and later. Then from Grenofen Bridge to the junction with the Tavy the angling is in private hands, though there are rumours that the Association will shortly acquire this right, and thus get possession of the whole stream. April and May are best for trout, with which the whole river is well stocked, while they run to a fair size and "pounders" are not very rare. The best flies are Blue Upright, Half-stone, Hare's Ear, Infallible, Cochybonddhu, Blue Dun, and Red Spinner. August and September are best for peal, most of which are accounted for by Devon and Phantom minnow. The total length of the Walkham is ten miles, as follows:|From source to Merivale, three miles; from Merivale to Huck- worthy, three miles; from Huckworthy to Horrabridge, one- and-a-half miles; from Horrabridge to Grenofen, one-and-a- half miles; from Grenofen to Junction, one mile.

The Tamar rises a few miles to the east of Bude, a seaport on the west coast of Cornwall. The early reports of the Fishery Inspectors give the length of its course as fifty- six miles, while the 1878 Report puts it at thirty-eight miles with a drainage area of three-hundred-and-eighty-five square miles, and this latter estimate, I think, is only some three orfour miles short of the actual course of the Tamar. The discrepancy is mentioned in no carping spirit, and I only regard it as a fact that will serve to hold me blameless if now and again I have made an error in my distances, for if Fishery Inspectors, who approach a river with all the prestige of the law at their backs, and with water bailiffs and keepers all anxious to help them, can yet make mistakes, then small wonder that I may do likewise with no such advantages in my favour.

The Tamar actually rises in Cornwall at Woolley Burrows, just across the Devon border, and in a short distance it becomes the march between the two counties and so remains for nearly the whole of its course.

Passing Tamerton at St. Stephen's by Launceston it is joined by the Werrington, to expand into a fine sheet of water in the park of that name; below this it is joined by the rapid-running Ottery. Then, at intervals passing under the bridges at Poulston and Greston and winding by the Endsleigh Woods, it has a tortuous run past Morwell, to expand into an estuary a little below Calstock, where for over a hundred years there has been a fishing weir. In 1822 the owner of it took 1,106 salmon:|June, 7 salmon; July, 28 salmon; August, 52 salmon; September, no; October, 480; November, 359; to i2th December, 70.

THE TAMAR AT ENDSLEIGH.

In 1829 only 300 were caught, and the lessee finding that all the breeding fish were being poached in the spawning beds, made a vigorous attack on the poachers, which bore good fruit, as in 1841 he netted 1,309 salmon, while the

VOL. I.

two following seasons were also good. Then the poaching began again, and was carried on by large gangs who defied the water bailiffs. This resulted in the gradual decrease of the fish, until in 1847 and '48 the lessee of the weir found himself out of pocket and finally in 1849 he retired.

In addition, however, to the poaching evil, the opening of the Devon Great Consols Copper Mine coincided with the fish scarcity, while at Latchley this Company erected a weir which was almost impassable. As the fishery below lacked a tenant, the Company then rented it for 30, though it had formerly been let for 160, and they did all they could to improve the fishing, both by carrying the fish above Latchley Weir and by sending their poisonous refuse into settling pits. The other mines of the district, fortunately for the fish, were situated so low down on the river that either they discharged their refuse into the estuary or into the tidal part, where the large and ever-changing body of water reduced the danger to a minimum. This state of affairs prevailed up to 1862, when the Fishery Commissioners found themselves confronted with pollutions, impassable weirs, and a dearth of fish ; and though the poachers had ceased to trouble only because there were no salmon to be poached, there was always the fear that any increase in the quantity of fish would surely result in a revival of their lawless proceedings.

In 1865, an Angling Association was formed for protecting the Tamar and its tributaries, the largest of which are the Inny and Lyd ; this was followed in 1866, by the formation of a Board of Conservators for the rivers Tamar, Tavy, Plym, Walkham, Lynher, and Yealm; water bailiffs were appointed and salmon rod licences issued at *JS. 6d.*

1867. 150 rod licences issued; very few salmon were caught, but sea trout were plentiful, chiefly in August and September.

1868. 167 rod licences issued; no records of sport. The Lynher reported as entirely destroyed, owing to the discharge of mineral refuse at the rate of 100 tons a week! This was formerly the best river in Cornwall.

1869. 200 salmon rod licences; mine pollutions other than Devon Great Consols much complained of. A good fish pass was placed in Latchley Weir.

1870. 128 salmon rod licences.

1871. 181 salmon rod licences; about 300 sea trout were caught in the district, chiefly in Tavy, none in Lynher.

1872. 166 salmon rod licences; a few salmon, largest 17 Ibs., and about 600 sea trout caught in district.

1873. 93 salmon rod licences; 12 salmon, and about 600 sea trout caught in the district. Open season for rods fixed to begin ist March and end 3ist October.

1874. 188 salmon rod licences; a few salmon and about 400 sea trout caught.

I75- 173 salmon rod licences ; a few salmon and between four and five hundred sea trout caught.

1876. 187 salmon rod licences; very few salmon; 800 sea trout caught.

1877. 162 salmon rod licences ; no reports.

1878. 209 salmon rod licences; 77 salmon and 43 sea trout caught in Tamar. 1,500 sea trout caught in Tavy and Walkham.

1879. 248 salmon rod licences. On Tavy and Walkham 53 rods took a few salmon and 1,116 sea trout.

1880. 230 salmon rod licences. A few salmon and upwards of 600 sea trout were caught by a portion of the licencees, but in this year as in the previous one there were so many rods at work that it was not possible to get full returns.

1881. 251 salmon rod licences. A very good rod season, but no accurate returns were made.

1882. 310 salmon rod licences. A very good season.

1883. 279 salmon rod licences. Open time for nets fixed from ist February to 3ist August, for rods from ist July to 2nd November. Anglers were allowed to carry the gaff all the season, but were expected to "tail" and returnkelts. Fresh run salmon were entering the river in April, but not in any great number.

1884. 279 salmon rod licences. No returns.

1885. 249 ,, A very dry season.

1886. 276 ,, ,, ,, No returns.

The turbines from some of the manufactories were reported as killing large quantities of fry. There is no doubt that they did.

1887. 187 salmon rod licences; a very poor angling season.

1888. 218 salmon rod licences; no records.

1889. 208 salmon rod licences. A Tin Mining Company was successfully prosecuted for poisoning the fish of the Walkham.

1890. 220 salmon rod licences.

1891. 240 salmon rod licences. A good angling season but no returns.

1892. 250 salmon rod licences.

1893. 2J6 salmon rod licences. The Conservators reported that large quantities of all kinds of fish were from time to time destroyed in the estuary by the explosion of Government mines when making experiments.

1894. 24 rd licences. The mine pollution was consider ably diminished owing to some of them ceasing to work.

i |

1895. 24 salmon rod licences.

1896. 247

1897. 279

1898. 221

1899. 237

1900. 251

1901. 199

1902. 210 salmon rod licences; Licence duty raised to *los.* The Duke of Bedford erected, at his own expense, a new fish pass at Latchley Weir; His Grace owns the angling from Greystone Bridge to the tideway and has bred large quantities of " Rainbows," which have spread themselves all over the river; they were turned in at Endsleigh, and Colonel Eagles took eleven of them one day when fishing ten miles above there ; he speaks of them as a sport-giving fish, much superior to the local trout, but as he returned them all to the water he is unable to vouch for their edible qualities. The Duke preserves his salmon fishing strictly and leave for a day is rarely granted, but though considerable numbers of salmon enter the river they do not lay hold of any lures as freely as they might be expected to do, and consequently the captures by rod are not in proportion to the number of fish that can be seen. With regard to the Tavy, Walkham and Plym Fishing Association, it is cer-

tainly one of the best managed clubs in the Kingdom: the subscription is as follows:|For the season, over all their waters, I *is. 6d.;* for the Cad, 5$.; for the Walkham, *2S. 6d. ;* for the Tavy to junction with Walkham, 55. ; day cards, *is.*

Trout season, ist March to 3Oth September; salmon, ist March to ist November; no angling allowed between 10 o'clock in the evening until 6 o'clock the following morning. No Sunday angling permitted. No wading allowed in the Tavy or in the Walkham up to Huckworthy Bridge. Artificial baits are only permitted in the Tavy below Marytavy Clam; in the Walkham below the weir next above Huckworthy Bridge; in the Meavy only below Nosworthy Bridge. Considering that this Association preserves between sixty and seventy miles of water the subscription is wonderfully moderate, and with a view of restocking and better preservation it might well be increased. The Secretary is Mr. W. W. Mathews, Solicitor, Tavistock. Salmon rod licence is *los.*; trout rod licence, *2s. 6d.*

The Chairman of Board of Conservators is Captain R. C. Coode, Polapit Tamar. *Clerk:* Mr. W. W. Mathews, Tavistock.

For much of my information about these rivers I am indebted to Colonel H. C. Eagles, of the Royal Marine Light Infantry, who has frequently fished them all.

10

SECTION 10

Chapter X
THE FOWEY

With a course of twenty-seven miles and a catchment basin of one hundred and seventeen square miles, rises in Bodmin Moor from the slopes of Brown Willy, one of Cornwall's highest hills. Flowing by St. Cleer and St. Neot, between which places it is sometimes called the Dreynes River, with a rapid - running broken stream, it turns to the south-westand passing Bodmin Road Station and Lanhydrock House, it meets the tide half-a-mile above Lostwithiel, the " Uzella" of Ptolemy. In 1867 the depression in the mining industry forced many mines to cease work, which brought better times to the *salmonicUe* of the river, though, prior to that, pollution had nearly wiped them all out, and so bad was the state of affairs that only one netting licence and not a single rod licence was issued. Up till the Act of 1861 salmon netting began on September ist and ended at Christmas, October and November being the best months.

THE ESTUARY OF THE FOWEY.

The fishermen complained loudly of the alteration of this close time, and urged strongly that the old one should be once more reverted to, or otherwise they would be reduced to starvation. As a test some fish were netted between October *gth* and i6th and sent to Mr. Buckland, the Fishery Inspector, for examination, who reported that " the external appearance of these Fowey fish corresponded with the condition of their ovaries and milts, that the fish were plump and fat and could not be called unclean or out of season : that their ova corresponded with those that had been taken from fish six and seven weeks previously from other and earlier rivers. Thus a few fish of 14 Ibs. taken from the Severn on August 2oth contained eggs weighing nine ounces; a Wye fish of 4th August contained eggs weighingeight ounces, while a fish of 8 Ibs. of October 2oth from Torridge had twenty-six ounces of eggs; of the specimen fish sent from the Fowey a male of the I4th October had eight- and-a-half ounces of milt, a female of the same date of 7 Ibs. only had five ounces of eggs. Mr. Buckland, therefore, suggested that the Fowey should be netted later than the 3151 August. At this period the river also suffered much from the washings of the china clay works, which is simply a solution of decomposed granite. There were then only three obstructions on the Fowey : the first at Treverbyn Mills, the second at the Golitha Falls, and the third at Ashford Weir. In 1867 a Board of Conservators was formed and most of the riparian owners interested themselves in the improvement of the river, notably Mr. R. Foster, who was Chairman of the Board, Mr. W. Pease of Lostwithiel, and Mr. Chapel

Hodge of Doublebois. In

1868. 8 salmon rod licences were issued at 5. and some 15 salmon and sea trout were got, and about 120 others were netted.

1869. No record.

1870. 23 rod licencees took 4 salmon, about 220 netted. The mine industry began to recover, but the owners did what they could to avoid pollution by making catch pits for their refuse.

1871. 19 rod licencees got 24 fish, also 60 were netted.

1872. 16 rod licencees got 24 fish. The deposits from the china clay works did great harm to the river by converting the natural gravel of the spawning beds into mere reaches of mud. The fishermen again complained bitterly of the hardships inflicted on them by not being allowed to net after the 3ist August : before that date became law six seine nets employing a good many men worked at the fishing till Christmas day, and the price they got ranged from *6d.* to *$d.* a pound, as in those days there was no railway to London. One fisher stated that he took out a licence in 1871 and, catching only 20 salmon, he was much out of pocket and that others were in the same plight.

1873. 6 rod licencees took n fish, and 600 were netted, but I am in some doubt if this is not an error and that the Report should read 60, not 600.

1874. ii rod licencees took 15 fish, and 100 were netted.

1875. No rod licences ; no returns.

1876. 26 rod licencees took 480, nearly all sea trout ; about 70 salmon and 450 sea trout netted.

1877. 35 rod licences; no reports.

1878. 35 rod licencees took a large number of sea trout. Licences raised from 5. to *'js. 6d.*

1879. 48 rod licences; price raised from *"js. 6d.* to 105.

1880. 42 rod licences ; open season for nets ordered to be from 3151 March to 3ist October, not to apply to any part of the river above Lostwithiel Bridge.

1881. 42 rod licences at *Ids. ;* no report.

1882. 45 ,, ,, ,,

I8S3- 55 ,, ,, ,,

1884. 25 ,, ,, ,,

1885. 50

1886. 79

1887. 70

1888. 72

1889. 89 ,, Trout licence raised from 35. to 5$.

1890. 51 rod licences at *los. ;* no report. The discharges from the mines of Tregeagle and Treveddoe made the river so dirty that fly fishing was hopeless.

1891. 80 rod licences. The Tregeagle mine, which was the worst offender, luckily for the fish and for the anglers, stopped work.

1892. 68 rod licences; a season of great drought.

1893. 47 rd licences; also very dry season.

1894. 36 rod licences. As the fishermen still complained of not being permitted to net in November and December, on the gth and loth January Mr. C. E. Fryer, the Inspectorof Fisheries netted 3 salmon which were declared by the men to be in excellent condition ; of these, two had partly spawned and the third was in the act of so doing, which clearly showed that the condition of fish was not such as would warrant netting to be carried on in December. I&95- ?6 rd licences ; no reports.

1896. 98 rod licences; river very low all the season. No mine refuse, as some had ceased to work, and the others had provided settling tanks.

1897. 118 rod licences; no reports.

1898. 98 ,, ,, ; a very dry season.

1899. 117

1900. 131 ,, ,, ; price raised from iOi. to 15.

1901. 51 rod licences at *is.,* 89 at *los.;* trout licences, 367 at 35., 178 at 55.

1902. 54 salmon licences at 155.; 403 trout at *$s.* Salmon and sea trout ascend the Fowey as far as Golitha Falls, a distance of about thirteen miles, and there are only brown trout above these Falls. Waders are not absolutely necessary, though stockings are useful for crossing the stream to get a better command of the different casts, while a rod of 12 ft. will cover all the water. Pools are numerous but small, and the banks in some places densely wooded. From Lostwithiel Bridge to Bodmin Road Station (with the excep-

VOL. I.

tion of perhaps half-a-mile in Lanhydrock Wood) Lord Clifden allows anyone to fish. Above Bodmin Road permission must be got from the landowners ; some of the best pools are the Bathing Pool, Wool Washing, Mine, Clam, Woodpecker, Drum, Turn, and Five Elms, with the Iron Mine Pool below Bodmin Bridge.

The largest and best sea trout, averaging about 3 Ibs., are caught from the opening of the season to July, and Mr. Robert Pease of Lostwithiel holds the record for the

river with a splendid trout of 14 Ibs. ; then come the school peel of about f Ibs. and
a few salmon if the water is sufficiently high. Bull trout appear towards the end of
August, followed by a run of autumn salmon, though of late years back-end angling
has been a failure. All the ordinary medium sized standard patterns of salmon flies
will kill, and sea trout take them when used smaller, also the Alexandra, the Silver
Doctor, and a fly with a yellow body, gold twist, Cochybonddhu hackle, with mottled
brown turkey wing and for tail a sprig of gold pheasant ruff, kills very well, a common
pattern on most of the Scotch lochs, and which, so far as I know, is nameless. Sizes
4 to 7 Limerick hooks. Prawn and worm are used for salmon, and Devon minnow for
sea trout. Before October salmon average 9 Ibs.. and after that they run as heavy as
25 Ibs. and have been taken up to35 Ibs. in the nets. For those parts of the river above
Bodmin Road most of the proprietors give permits for the season to their friends, or
for one or two days a week, and this is the best part of the river, as the free water
below, like all other free waters, is very hard fished, though on no part of the river do
more than half-a-dozen salmon and grilse fall to one rod. After heavy rains in July
and August the river keeps in flood for about twenty-four hours, and then fishers of the
worm and the Devon minnow kill many sea trout, with a few salmon. A friend who
has fished the river for many years writes to me as follows :l" Years ago the Fowey
was a good salmon river, but can now hardly be called so at all; every season they
seem to be scarcer and to run later, and the greater number of them do not appear on
the spawning beds till close on Christmas. In years gone by October and November
were the best months, but last season (1902) though there was plenty of water, I did
not hear of a single salmon being killed in these months. The biggest fish I have seen
in the river was a few winters ago, an apparently fresh run cock fish which had been
killed by an otter and weighed 34 Ibs. The Fowey, however, is still an excellent peel
or sea trout river, and in August in low water I have often seen several hundreds in one
pool, of from i to 3 Ibs., but except when the river is in flood they feed only atnight,
when the best lure is a rather large Alexandra; it is not unusual for one rod to get from
fifteen to twenty in two or three hours. Lately most of the riparian owners, who are
very generous in granting permits, have prohibited night fishing, though I am sorry to
say it is still carried on to a great extent in the open water, for I think it tends to make
the peel unduly shy during the day. The fly I send you (already described as a Scotch
Loch fly) is the best for the water, and a professional fisher in ten evenings last August
killed with it over 60 peel and 2 salmon."

Here is a silly story, but true all the same ; it only tends to show how greatly the
weight of a lost fish can increase in the imagination of the unlucky angler. In August,
1901, an aged local fisher hooked a salmon of about 15 Ibs. in the Wheel Pit Pool,
and when several vain attempts had been made to land it Couch, the water bailiff,
appeared on the scene, and quickly gaffing it, duly knocked it on the head, while the
two then stood admiring their victim. "Well, he's the biggest I've killed this season;
what weight do you judge him ?" exclaimed the old angler, " Oh! somewhere about
15 Ibs. !" said Couch, "Well, I do hope it will be 16 Ibs., for that will make it the
heaviest I've ever killed!" replied the ancient one. At that moment the fish, which had
only been stunned and not killed, gave a great flop, and ereeither of them could get
hold of it it slid down the grassy bank, to vanish for ever, to the accompaniment of

language which will not bear repeating. Last season I happened to meet this unlucky old angler on the identical pool, when naturally the incident became the subject of conversation. "What a pity! and a nice fish of 15 Ibs., too," said I. " Fifteen pounds did you say, sir! why I will take my davy it was nearer thirty than twenty-five!" cried the ancient angler. Poor old fellow, he quite believed it.

The close time for nets is from November ist to 4th April ; for rods from ist December to 4th April, but between Lostwithiel Bridge and a line drawn from north end of Penquite Wood to St. Winnow Point from December ist to April 3Oth.

Chairman of Board of Conservators: Mr. G. P. S. Glencross, Luxstone, Liskeard. *Clerk:* Mr. W. Pease Junior, Lostwithiel. To these two gentlemen and to Mr. H. J. Rowse of Carwogie, St. Columb, I am much indebted for the greater part of my information.

11

SECTION 11

Chapter XI
THE CAMEL

Is a river with an eccentric course of some twenty-eight miles, and a catchment basin of 155 square miles; for, rising in the north part of Cornwall, only some five miles from the sea and about opposite Tintagel Head, it flows due south for nearly twenty miles, and passing Camelford and St. Tucly a little to the west of Bodmin, it takes a sharp turn to the N.N.W., to expand five miles further on into an estuary at Egloshayle and Wadebridgela long narrow sheet of water known as Padstow Harbour. In 1863, poaching was prevalent, for twenty-three men paid fines, and lost three boats with 356 yards of net; also two spears and fifty salmon were taken from them. The pollutions from tin mines were fast destroying the river, their owners would not hear of intercepting pits, while the workmen declared that either the river must remain polluted to the entire destruction of the fish, or that the mines must cease work for the benefit of the salmon.

At Bodmin there was a nearly impassable weir for the supply

K

DQ

X

H

of the town waterworks, while below this at Boscarne Mills there was another impediment nearly as bad.

Prior to the Act of 1861, the netting season used to be from ist September to Christmas Day, and when the close time was altered by the 1861 Act, the fishers called it "the Act to prohibit catching and eating salmon in Cornwall." In addition to the poison from the tin mines, the river also had to contend against the deposits of several china day- works. This was the state of affairs in 1866, when a Board of Conservators was formed, funds were raised by the sale of licences, and the riparian owners promised their support, while Mr. W. R. Gilbert so improved the pass in Bodmin Weir that many fish ascended it. In this year the nets caught about 60 salmon, with numerous sea trout. The rods did not get many, but 54 licences were issued at §*s.*

1870. 47 salmon rod licences; no records; a very dry season.

1871. 45 salmon rod licences ; no records, but an average season.

1872. No reports ; as the weir at Bodmin still remained a great obstruction it was proposed to tunnel round it.

1873. It was decided that netting was to be continued during September, and that rods could fish to 15th November. A great part of the Waterworks Weir was washed away, andsteps were taken to ensure a proper fish pass when the weir was rebuilt. 20 salmon averaging 20 Ibs. were netted; 5 salmon averaging 20 Ibs., taken by rod.

1874. 19 rod licences; nets took 15 salmon and 600 peel; rods took 12 salmon and 100 peel.

J875. 13 rod licences ; nets took 10 salmon and about 900 peel; rods took close on 200 peel.

1876. 4 rod licences ; takes of nets and rods about the same as previous year.

1877. 20 rod licences; nets took 12 salmon and 2,900 peel of one pound each ; rods took 200 peel.

1878. 30 rod licences; nets took 12 salmon and 2,900 peel ; rods took 250 peel.

1879. 24 rod licences ; duty raised from 55. to *los.* Nets to commence ist May and fish till ist November ; rods to begin ist May and fish till ist December.

1880. 19 rod licences ; no reports. As many fish passed up Bodmin Weir, the spawning beds above were cleansed by manual labour from the china clay deposits, as the gravel had become so hard set as to be immovable by the fish.

1881. 10 rod licences; no reports.

1882. 18

1883. 26

1884. 26 A very dry summer.1885. 23 rod licences ; no reports.

1886. 36 rod licences; no reports; great complaints of poaching near Padstow by small-mesh nets, nominally fishing for sea fish, also much poaching from the spawning beds a few miles below Camelford.

1887. 26 rod licences; no reports; a very dry summer and many fish poached by groping.

1888. 29 rod licences; no reports; The new fish pass in Bodmin Weir was a failure.

1889. 32 rod licences; no reports.

1890. 33 rod licences ; anglers in the upper waters had good peel fishing.

1891. 31 rod licences; no reports.

1892. 33 rod licences; the Bodmin Waterworks Co. was ordered under a penalty of .$300 to construct a weir and maintain a fish pass within six months.

1893. 26 rod licences; no reports; Close season for salmon netting to begin 2ist September instead of ist November.

1894. 23 rod licences; no reports; licence duty raised from *i os.* to *2S.* and for trout only from 3$. to 4. A conviction was obtained against the Bodmin Waterworks Co. and they forfeited $300 to the Conservators.

1895. 21 rod licences at *izs. ;* no reports.

1896. 19 rod licences at 125.; no reports.

1897. J6 rod licences at *12s.* ; no reports; disease appeared and more than 20 dead salmon, chiefly cocks, were removed from the river.

1898. 31 rod licences at *12s. ;* no reports; the Bodmin Weir fish pass approved by the Board of Trade.

1899. 27 rod licences; no reports.

1900. 21 rod licences; no reports; it was decided to issue fortnightly salmon rod licences at 5., weekly ones *2s. 6d.,* and day *is.*

1901. 15 rod licences, 12., 10 at *$s.,* 5 at 15.; a very dry season, rod take below average.

1902. 25 licences at *izs.,* 19 fortnight at 5$., 173 for trout at 4.!?., 31 fortnight at *25. 6d.,* 58 day at *is. ;* rod fishing good.

If there is good water in June peel run freely all the month and vary in weight from ij to 3 Ibs., while some are taken up to 5 Ibs. In July, 1901, one rod had ten in two days. The school peel run in September, while October and November are the best salmon months, as this river, with the Fowey, are the two latest ones in England. There are no rules as to carrying a gaff, and the flies and lures that kill on the Fowey will be effective here. In the upper parts of the river the pools are deep, with big bouldersinterspersed between them and in some places the trees are much too thick for comfortable casting. In the season of 1902 only a few salmon were caught by rod, six or seven in all, certainly under a dozen. Nets commence 5th April and come off on 2Oth September. The size of mesh measured when wet must not exceed inches from knot to knot ; a 2-inch mesh would be better, as a smaller one takes smolts and school peel. Rod fishing for salmon begins ist May and ends 3Oth November. Trout fishing commences 16th March and ends 3Dth September.

The greater part of the river is free, and, even where it is not open to the public, applications are seldom refused. There is also the River Camel Fishing Association, with Mr. Ellis, Wadebridge, as Hon. Secretary.

Chairman of Board of Conservators: Mr. J. J. E. Venning, Devonport. *Clerk:* Mr. G. L. Ellis, Solicitor, Wadebridge.

12

SECTION 12

Chapter XII
THE TORRIDGE AND TAW.

The Torridge has even a more eccentric course than the Camel, for rising near the little village of Meddon, and within a few miles of the sea coast of Bude Bay, it at first flows in a tortuous course mainly due south, and then veering to the east at Bradford, it flows to the Okement Junction, where it turns sharply to the north, and passing Beaford and Torring- ton, it meets the tide at Wear Gifford, a few miles below which is Bideford, with Instow at the estuary mouth. With a total length of about thirty-five miles, and a catchment basin of 350 square miles, it forms a common estuary with the Taw, which falls in at Barnstaple.

In 1861 the nets in the estuary were worked all the year round by about twenty boats, while during October and several months later large quantities of salmon were consigned to London, *en route* for Paris. The whole river, as well as the Okement tributary, was obstructed with "Browse Weirs," while at Monk Okehampton there was an impassable weir of stone.

No sooner was the close time of the 1861 Act enforcedthan clean fish were taken by rod above Bram Weir or Wear Gifford, which up till then had been unheard of, and altogether upwards of 80 fish were caught by anglers, one of them having as many as 42 to his own rod.

See Taw for description.

THE TORRIDGE AT TADO1PORT BRIDGE, TORR1NGTOM.

In 1863 this remarkable improvement was continued, a Conservator getting 45 fish to his own rod, while the take of the nets increased so much that the price of salmon fell from 25. a pound to 15., and for a short time it was as low as %d. in Barnstaple and Bideford.

In 1864 there were two Angling Associations formed, which sold tickets at a profit, that was spent on better preservation, but up to this time there was no licence duty on nets or rods.

1866. A proper Board of Conservators was formed, who fixed the sums to be paid for licences for nets and rods.

1867. 166 salmon rod licences issued at *los. 6d.* each. A few clean fish were caught in May above Dolton Weir.

1868. 165 rod licences issued, and a few clean fish were caught as early as March. The estuary boats made a clear profit of from *$60* to ,$70 each, and it was estimated that between them they took about 4,000 fish of 10 Ibs. each. A very dry summer spoilt the rod fishing.

On the Torridge and its tributaries there are close on 75 weirs, most of them " browse weirs," and the rest stone built, and many of them impassable.

1869. 197 rod licences issued at *Iqs. 6d.* ; according to the Fishery Board Reports at *js. 6d.*|probably a printer's error. A very dry season interfered with angling.

1870. 142 rod licences. A very poor season all round.

1871. 172 rod licences. Also a very poor season.

1872. 143 rod licences. On the middle reaches 21 salmon, 19 sea trout, and 5 bull trout were caught by rod, the water bailiff reporting that he had no means of ascertaining the captures made in the lower waters.

1873. 176 rod licences.

1874. No reports.

1875. 146 rod licences.

1876. 151 rod licences; no reports.

1877. 162

1878. 176

1879. 192

1880. 205

1881. 184

1882. 231

In this season a considerable increase of salmon was observed, which, it may be presumed, had been in gradual progress since 1876, or otherwise the number of licences would not have increased so steadily. On the other hand, there was a marked decrease in migratory trout, which was attributed, and probably rightly, to the mesh of the estuary nets having been reduced to one of six inches : the smaller mesh held the floating seaweed, and so choked it up that the nets caught very small fish. The old mesh had been one of eight inches round when wet, or two inches from knot to knot.

1883. 234 rod licences; drought quite spoilt everything; we heard of good netting.

1884. 187 rod licences; very dry.

1885. 169 rod licences; great complaint was made by the anglers that the estuary nets swept up nearly the whole of the sea trout, and were able to catch them of less than a pound in weight. A memorial signed by 130 riparian owners and anglerswas presented to the Secretary of State praying for a return to the 8-inch mesh. Hardly any sea trout were caught by the rod.

1886. It was estimated that about 60 salmon were got by the Torridge rods.

1887. 165 rod licences; poor angling season; some disease noticed. The estuary nets increased from 42 to 50, a certain sign that the industry was a profitable one.

1888. 167 rod licences; duty raised from *los.* to *2OS.* Fair summer sport; none in autumn. The 8-inch mesh was re-established.

1889. 123 rod licences at *2os.;* no reports.

1890. 117 *20s.*;

1891. 136 20. ;

1892. 122 *2is.;*

1893. 127 *2is.;*

1894. 114 *2is.;*

I&95- 95 rod licences at 21.; the rods took above the average number of salmon, and much below it of sea trout; disease was bad in the spring; nets did well.

1896. 92 rod licences; above the average for salmon with rod.

1897. 105 rod licences; fortnightly ones for salmon issued at 10.

1898. 83 rod licences at 20.; 32 ditto at *los.*

1899. 77 rod licences at 20$. ; 16 ditto at icw. ; a very bad season all round.

1900. 69 rod licences at 215.; 25 ditto at icw. ; it was announced that the income of the Board of Conservators was insufficient to meet the expenditure.

1901. 85 rod licences issued at 24.; fortnightly licences abolished; good season for nets ; too dry for sport with rod.

1902. 93 rod licences at *245.*

In the account of the Taw which follows, it will be seen that no mention is made of the number of rod licences issued, as those given above are the total number of licences issued for the two rivers. They are nearly equally divided, but, perhaps, there are six issued to the Torridge anglers against five to those of the Taw. The returns of the last six years show that the licences have averaged 85 each year, and if 45 fished the Torridge and 40 the Taw, no cry of over- fishing can fairly be raised, which might, perhaps, have been the case in 1883, when no less than 234 rod licences were issued for the Taw and the Torridge at icxy. each.

The chief proprietors are Lord Clinton, the Hon. Mark Rolle, Mr. J. T. Smyth Osbourne, Mr. R. Preston Whyte, Mr. C. M. Saunders, Mr. Coham Fleming, Major VVendd, Mr. E. J. Oldham, General Halley, and Major R. A. Moore- Stevens. Salmon are taken as far up as Dippe's Mills.

VOL. I.

April is the best month for spring fish ; for sea trout the first flood after the aoth June usually gives the best sport. Jock Scott, Butcher, and Silver Doctor are the local favourites, but I think any of the standard patterns have almost as good a chance. The

Devon minnow used from a Nottingham reel is also a favourite lure ; sea trout take this pretty freely, as

TOWN MILLS BRIDGE, NEAR TORRINGTON.

well as small salmon flies. Spring fish average 10 Ibs. and autumn ones 17 Ibs. The dry summers that have prevailed so frequently of late years are the angler's chief bugbear, though, of course, the estuary nets take a very heavy|perhaps an unduly heavy|toll of all fish coming to the river, a toll that would be lessened if the recommendation of the 1902Commission were accepted, and the weekly close time lengthened from 42 to 48 hours. The District Board of Conservators is somewhat a large one, as there are no less than thirty-three members, and as the total length of the Taw and Torridge is about one hundred miles, of which only about sixty-six miles is salmon water, there is a member for every two miles of river, which has always made it a matter of difficulty to fix any particular meeting day to suit each individual. The gaff may not be used before the ist of June. Netting commences on ist May and continues to 20th September. Rods begin ist April and can be plied to November i5th. Mr. J. M. Pope, of Spence Combe, Copplestone, is *Chairman of Board of Conservators,* and Mr. W. H. Toller, Solicitor, Barnstaple, is *Clerk.*

THE TAW

Is about fifty miles in length, with a catchment basin of four hundred and fifty-five square miles. The first weir above the mouth at Umberleigh is owned by the Hon. Mark Rolle and Mr. C. H. Barrett, though there are many others above, as well as on the fine tributary The Mole. Their construction is peculiar and locally called " Browse Weirs "; they consist of brushwood with the thick ends laid up stream, boundtogether with wattles and then covered for many feet thick with clay, stones and rubbish, while the twigs and branches projected out over the surface of the pool below the weir in such a manner as to entirely prevent fish from approaching the fall, and thus, except when floods were so heavy as to raise the water below the weir to the same level as the river above, it was almost impossible for fish to pass up; while, moreover, in 1860 nearly all the weirs had fish traps in them, which caught alike clean and unclean fish as well as most of the smolts.

Tawhead itself is on Dartmoor, near Cranmere Pool, and after the stream has passed North and South Tawton and Nymet Rowland it is joined by that good trout tributary the Yeo; from there it flows past Eggesford, and is shortly joined by the Little Dart, with Lee House at the junction; then a few miles further on it receives the Mole, and in another twelve miles or so it reaches Barnstaple.

In 1862 a Board of Conservators was formed, who at once directed their energies to restricting the estuary netting to the open time, for up till then it had been carried on nearly all the year round. A fish pass was placed in Umberleigh Weir and Earl Fortescue made another one on the Mole Weir; this resulted in salmon being taken by rod above Umberleigh, which had never before occurred within the memory of the oldest natives ; 40 salmon were caught bythe rods, while in one day two anglers had 47 sea trout where none had ever been caught before.

In 1864 two Angling Associations were formed. The Board of Conservators, however, broke up, as subscriptions fell off to only ,$30 a year, the upper proprietors stating that they had no intention of paying their money for the sole benefit of the netsmen. In 1866 another Board was formed and net and rod licences were imposed, the former having increased from 21 nets in 1860 to 37, each requiring a boat and from three to five men.

1868. A few clean fish were caught in February, though the chief run is June, July and August.

1869. A very dry summer. The rods took between 60 and 70 fish in October.

1870. A very bad season all through and there were hardly any autumn fish.

1871. In September and October 22 salmon were taken in the Taw and Mole, and about the same number from the opening day to the end of August. In the Bray tributary 8 fish were caught in the whole season.

1872. 21 fish caught in Taw, 33 in Mole and 3 in Bray.

1873. Taw and Mole yielded 60 fish of 9 Ibs. averagel chiefly grilse.

1874. Taw yielded 39 fish. Mole 28.

VOL. I.

1875. No reports.

1876.

1877.

1878. Open time for nets fixed from ist May to 2oth September; for rods from ist April to i6th November.

1879. No reports.

1880.

1881.

1882. There was an increase in salmon this year, but a great decrease of migratory trout.

1883. A great netting season ; a long drought entirely spoilt angling.

1884. A very dry season.

1885. A heavy run of autumn salmon.

1886. 193 rod licences issued for the district, at *los. 6d.* On the Taw and tributaries 124 fish were captured.

1887. No reports.

1888. 167 rod licences for the district ; the cost was raised from *los.* to 20. A bad season ; one rod had a dozen fish, but no other took as many. A sea trout angler at work every day got 60 sea trout, and no one else took nearly that quantity.

1889. There were increased numbers of sea trout ; salmon snatching in close time was very prevalent.

1890. A very poor season.

1891. An average season ; sea trout appeared in larger numbers ; a few clean fish taken by rods in April. Ordered that no gaff be carried in the district before ist June.

1892. No records.

1894.

1895. Exceptionally good netting in estuary ; rods caught more than an average number of salmon, but fewer sea trout.

1896. Below the average for nets and rods.

1897. It was resolved to issue fortnightly salmon rod licences at Iqj.

1898. No reports.

1899. A bad season all round.

1900. Rod licences raised to 245., and the fortnightly licence was abolished.

1901. Good net fishing; very poor angling. Nearly the whole river is in private hands. April is the best month for spring fish, which average about 10 lbs., while those of the autumn average 17 lbs. ; grilse do not ascend in any quantity ; for peel the best time is the first flood after midsummer. The favourite flies are Jock Scott, Butcher, and Silver Doctor, sizes from o for big water, down to 8 for sea trout ; Limerick hooks. The Devon minnow is also much used. The bigsea trout begin to run at the end of May, the school peel coming later and continuing to run till the end of September.

To the kindness of my friend, Mr. H. Vaughan Clark of Ridgewood, near Bristol, I am indebted for the excellent photos of the Taw, as well as for *a.* particularly correct account of the river round about South Molton Road, and as Mr. Vaughan Clark has fished this part of it regularly for upwards of ten years, better information could not be desired Nearly the whole of the fishings of the Taw and Mole are in private hands and in most cases strictly preserved, though in a few instances angling can be had by staying at small, but clean and comfortable inns, where the charges are most moderate. To begin from the top of the river, the first fishing of any note is that which goes with the " Fox and Hounds" at Eggesford, where the angling rights for some miles above the inn belong to the landlord, and are free to his guests ; here in many places the river is thickly bushed, and wading stockings are necessary; the spring trouting is very fair, and from two to three dozen a day may be caught, though they will not average more than five to the pound.

Late in the autumn, if there have been floods, an occasional salmon may also be caught, for a few yards below the inn there is a small weir which fish are seldom able to surmount, unless there have been exceptionally high floods ;therefore it may be said that above Eggesford there is no salmon fishing. Below the weir, for about a mile-and-a-half, with about the same extent on the Little Dart, the angling is let to a Fishing Association, but the landlord of the " Fox and Hounds " can issue tickets at a very small cost. Eggesford Weir Pool often holds salmon, though they are not much fished for ; the village schoolmaster used to work it regularly with a Devon minnow, whenever the water was right, and he usually took about a dozen salmon each season. Indeed the Taw, until it joins the Mole, is nothing much of a salmon river, for many of the pools are muddy and full of large dace, and I doubt if there are 20 salmon a year killed above the Mole Junction.

After a spate the single Taw, as the natives call it above the junction, takes some time to clear, whilst the Mole, with its more rapid and clearer water, fines down very quickly. Though perhaps not more than 20 salmon a season are killed above the Mole Junction, yet many peel ascend the single Taw and good takes are made each year, chiefly in the Little Dart, which, like the Mole, also clears very quickly. At South Molton Road the " Fortescue Arms " has about a mile of the single Taw on the right bank, which of late years has not yielded so many salmon as formerly; the hotel water goes right to the Junction Pool, and turns upthe left bank of the Mole for about a mile. The Junction Pool is large and deep, and never without salmon, though they are not free takers. The Mole joins the Taw at right angles, and with its cleaner and more rapid running water, it may be said that nineteen out of every twenty running fish prefer it to the Taw. Except in times of floods very little can be done without wading trousers, and with these the best part of the Junction Pool can be fished from the hotel side. About a mile up the Mole comes Head Bridge, and then about a quarter of a mile higher up comes Head Weir, which is made with logs of wood arranged in steps, with a good salmon pass up the centre. The King's Nympton Park fishing begins at Head Bridge, and is the best water on the whole river, though perhaps now that the Browse Weir, some mile-and-a-half higher up, has been washed away, the fish may not rest so long as usual; prior to that, the beautiful chain of pools below it were full of fish, the Weir Pool itself being literally packed with them, and it was not unusual for one rod to get from six to twelve fish a day with minnow and prawn. This fine stretch of water is let with King's Nympton House. Above this comes three miles of most perfect salmon and trout water, rented on long lease by Mr. Durn and the Rev. I Thorould. At the top of this angling the Bray joins the Mole ; both

Mr. H. VAUGHAN CLARK ON THE BOTTOMLESS POOL.

THE GARDEN POOL.

salmon and peel push their way up to the head waters, where many are poached by the Exmoor shepherds. Mr. Vaughan Clark's best day on the Mole was in the spring of 1889, when he got five fish, ranging from 6 to iOj Ibs., on a Jock Scott; and on another day, when trouting in most unfavourable weather with two small Irish flies, Orange and Grouse and " Orange Rail," he got three dozen, which weighed exactly 10 Ibs. After a flood the Taw and the Mole keep in order for about three days, at the end of which time all keen anglers start praying for more rain, and, if none comes, a small sea trout fly on fine gut is the best chance of a fish. To return to the Double Water, as they style the Taw below the Mole Junction, the last mile of the right bank of the Mole, with many miles of the right bank of the Taw, is owned by the Hon. Mark Rolle, who preserves strictly, though not an angler himself. He generally grants a limited number of free tickets to his friends and his tenants, and as once granted they are rarely cancelled, they are eagerly sought after, though they must be renewed each year. Mr. Rolle also owns a large stretch of the best angling on the Torridge, which he deals with in a like liberal manner. Some two or three years back the abuse of the minnow at some of the weirs led to an order that the fly only was to be used on Mr. Rolle's water.

The first angling on the left bank below the junction extends for one-and-a-half miles and has been let for the last three seasons to the " Fortescue Arms"; there are five large and good casts, of which perhaps the best is " The Rocks "; it should be mentioned that the bedroom accommodation of the

UMBERLEIGH BROWSE WEIR.

" Fortescue Arms" is limitedǀI think there are only threeǀ the charge for board, lodging and angling is but *los. 6d.* a day and the hotel is thoroughly comfortable. Below this Bridge Fishery comes two-and-a-half miles of excellent water which is rented by the three Messrs. Pope; then comes theAbbot's Marsh Fishery owned by Mr. I. M. Pope of Spence Combe, Copplestone, and Chairman of the Board of Conservators and a good keen angler. Below this the Hon. Mark Rolle owns and works a fish trap at Umberleigh Weir, a browse weir which in times of low water is a nasty obstruction, though of course the weekly close times are strictly observed.

There can be no doubt if the fish pass in this weir were improved and some further restriction placed on the estuary netting, that then the Taw would about equal the Usk for its rod fishing. The usual method of angling is Devon minnow and Nottingham reel; I cannot hear that anyone has tried the natural minnow with Dee tackle, which would probably prove more killing ; in the spring the fly is effective, particularly Jock Scott and the silver-bodied ones. In this wet autumn of 1903 fish have been plentiful throughout the river; the heaviest, of 26 Ibs., was taken with a Jock. Mr. Pope of Copplestone made an autumn record with five fish in one day, weighing 87 Ibs., all with the Devon; Mr. Vaughan Clark had fish of 20 and igf Ibs., one with Devon and the other with prawn, while many others were killed by the various anglers. The close times for nets and rods are the same as those of the Torridge, and so also are the Chairman of the Board and the Clerk.

13

SECTION 13

Chapter XIII
THE SEVERN

This, the second largest river in England, rises from the side of Plinlimmon on the borders of Cardiganshire and Montgomeryshire, with its source but a few miles from that of the Wye. Some twelve miles below its font it passes the flannel town of Llanidloes, and flowing thence in a north-easterly direction past Caersws and Newtown, after skirting Montgomery, at about Berriew it turns still more to the north, and then passing Welshpool and Llandrinio it enters Shropshire at Melverley, when after a very tortuous run of about twenty miles, mainly in an easterly direction, it reaches Shrewsbury where it bends nearly due south, and flowing by Wroxeter, Leighton and Buildwas Abbey it arrives at Ironbridge, from whence it hurries on to Bridgnorth and Kidderminster after having entered the county of Worcester a few miles above the carpet town ; from there it flows in a broad stream for about fifteen miles until it reaches Worcester, and a further run of about the same distance brings the river to Tewkes- bury, where it meets the tide. From there to Gloucester isabout the same distance, and from the Cathedral City it
    gradually widens out into a long narrow estuary, eventually

to expand into the Bristol Channel. The total length of
the Severn is variously estimated at from 180 to 200 miles,
with a drainage area of about 4,500 square miles; its length is made out approxi-
mately as follow:l

From source to Llanidloes ... ... about 12 miles.

From Llanidloes to the Montgomeryshire border ... 33

Through the County of Shropshire 65

Stourport to Worcester 14

Worcester to Tewkesbury ... ... 14 ,,

Tewkesbury to Gloucester 12

Gloucester to Bello Pool, where the estuary begins ... 10

From Bello Pool to mouth of Bristol Avon 25

Its tributaries are numerous, but those of Montgomeryshire and above the Vrynwy
junction are but of little account as matters are at present, for few salmon ever reach
there. The Vrynwy, which falls in on the left bank at the Shropshire border, is a
very large tributary, which would become a fine breeding ground if there were fish
to stock it. Below this junction all the streams falling in on the left bank are useless
for spawning grounds, for salmon do not ascend there, while on the right bank there
is the Dowles Brook, a favourite spawning place, and joining the mainstream above
Bewdley. Then there is no other tributary of importance until the Teme falls in below
Worcester. In 1860 this pretty river was blocked by a weir at Powick only a few miles
above the junction, and so limited were the Severn spawning grounds at this time, and
so severe was the netting, that the salmon fisheries were at their lowest ebb.

The navigation weirs, of which there were five constructed in 1842, had done much
to ruin the river, as none of them were provided with efficient passes, while above
and below Shrewsbury there were also eel weirs, which were illegally fished in the
spring, solely for the capture of salmon smolts. The estuary was fished by "putts" and
"putchers," each shore being thickly studded with these engines, which were easily
erected and self-acting, also unlicenced and worked with a total disregard of all close
times ; enormous was the damage they did, while so long as the exertions of the upper
proprietors protected the spawners and increased the number of salmon, so *pari passu*
did these fixed engines multiply, and at this period it was estimated that between eight
and nine thousand "putts and putchers" were at work! By 1863 they had increased to
11,200!!

Then an Act of Parliament provided against any further increase, titles were closely
scrutinized and they were limited strictly to those that were lawfully exercised at the
time ofthe passing of the Act of 1861, and all those that could not produce Charters or
show usage from time immemorial were abolished; until by 1867 the Putts had been
reduced to 238, each working with a *2s. 6d.* licence, while the Putchers fell 4,680,
with a licence of *20s.* for each fifty. These putts and putchers are of great antiquity
and, when once set, will continue to catch by day and by night; a putcher or " butt," as
it is called on some parts of the estuary, is a conical- shaped wicker basket not unlike
the old strawberry pottle, it is about twenty-four inches in diameter at the mouth and
tapers nearly to a point; they are used chiefly for catching small fish and shrimps,
though they will also catch salmon and are regarded by the law as engines for taking

them : they are fixed in stages of tiers three, four or five above each other, and the largest fishery at Goldcliffe near the Usk mouth, which I think is the property of Eton College, holds *1,200* of them in one rank; their mouths are turned up stream so as to catch fish dropping back to the sea on the ebb tide, while close by there is another set of 900 laid with mouths down stream so as to catch fish coming up with the flood tide. Putts are too large to permit of being placed in tiers above one another, and are set in rows almost touching each other: they consist of three baskets, the outer one or "Knipe" being about six feet in diameter|some are rather

VOL. I.

less, some are rather more|the centre basket or putt is of smaller size, and the lower one called variably the " Diddle " and " Firewheel " comes nearly to a point, and these larger engines are used exclusively for catching salmon. Above Tewkesbury, where the tideway ends, there was a public right of fishing with nets up to Welshpool, a distance oF eighty-five miles. Clean fish were usually netted on the opening day, the 2nd of February, though the main harvest was in May, June and July, while grilse ran in June, July and August and the kelts have disappeared by the end of April.

There are in addition to the five navigation weirs very many others, close on thirty altogether, including those on the tributaries, with many small mill weirs in addition. At Gloucester there are the weirs of Maisemore and Llantony, then one at Tewkesbury, then Diglis Weir at Worcester while five miles higher is Bevere Weir and about the same distance above that is Holt, which is followed by Lincombe Weir a little below Stourport: then for upwards of fifty miles the river is free from obstruction until Pool Quay Weir comes, a little below Welshpool.. Then twenty miles further up there are in close proximity the weirs of Penarth, Glenhafron, and Milford, and further up at Llanidloes there is one more. On the Teme, a river of sixty-five miles, there are five weirs, viz., at Powick, Bramford, Knightwick, Hartley, and Stanford, with the impassable weir of Ashford above them. The upper proprietors of this river, with the fate of the upper proprietors of the Severn staring them in the face, are very antagonistic to the laddering of any of these weirs. The river as they have it yields splendid trout and grayling angling; fish which they can catch and keep for themselves, with much sport and amusement ; so, naturally, they say they would rather have this sport than spoil it by trying to breed salmon for the benefit of greedy netters below; and I think they are quite right. In addition to the evils already mentioned, the Severn suffered from the drainage pollutions of the large towns on its banks, as well as from the refuse of the carpet works, tanneries, and dye yards, and other manufactories, and in fact this fine river could hardly have fallen into a worse state than that in which the Act of 1861 found it. Prior to that, with a view of restoring the fisheries, most of the large towns on the banks had formed Protection Associations, whose efforts soon began to bear fruit, for in 1862 there was a larger number of salmon *netted* than for the thirty-five years previously; 350 were caught in the Shrewsbury district, while a fish was actually killed on the Teme by rod; the total take was valued at ;$i,ooo worth of fish at wholesale price. This trumpery yield was at that time a matter of congratulation until someonepointed out that the Tay in Scotland, which is only about half the size of the Severn, had that same year brought in a rental of .$14,000 for its salmon fishings. In 1866, a Board of Conservators was formed, and putts, putchers, nets, and rods, were all licenced ; for the latter there were 97 issued at *Iqs.* each, their united take being about 20 salmon!

In 1868 strenuous efforts were made by the Conservators to improve the fish passes in all the weirs. Eighteen salmon were taken by 70 rod licencees, while the netters withheld all information.

In 1869, 50 tons of salmon were reported as netted, or 11,150 *salmonida;* 73 rod licencees took 50 salmon.

1870. 22,500 salmon netted; 59 rod licencees took 12 salmon ; a very dry season.

1871. 16,870 netted; 38 rod licencees took 44 salmon.

1872. 6,500 netted; 33 rod licencees took 12 salmon.

1873. 10,400 netted; one of 64 Ibs. caught in a putcher ; 38 rod licencees caught 20 salmon. In this year the pollutions from Worcester and Gloucester and the Bewdley lanyards were very bad. It was also noticed that as salmon ascended to Shrewsbury they always took the west side of the river, but that after this point they invariably kept to the east side.

1874. 16,500 netted ; 43 rod licencees caught 16 salmon. Up to this period the average income of the Conservatorshad been *$620,* and of this .$480 per annum had been spent on protection ; it was stated at their Annual Meeting that out of 290 miles of spawning ground, only 75 miles were accessible to salmon.

1875. 14,650 netted; 43 rod licencees caught 12 salmon.

1876. 21,500 netted, averaging 14 Ibs., of which 20,050 were got in the tideway and estuary. 51 rod licencees caught 25 salmon averaging 10 Ibs. each.

1877. 18,400 netted; 46 rods caught 50 salmon.

1878. 12,450 netted ; 46 rods caught 58 salmon.

1879. 9,855 netted ; 56 rods caught 145 salmon, averaging 12 Ibs. each. 4,000 trout licences issued at *is.* each.

1880. 16,000 netted; 59 rods caught 15 salmon; 4,550 licences at *is.*

1 88 1. 19,500 netted; no returns made for rod and line.

1882. 15,450 netted; 40 rods caught 50 salmon n Ibs. average. At this period the close times were for nets from September ist to January 3ist ; for rods from November 2nd to January 3ist; for putts and putchers, September ist to April 30th.

1883. 30,000 netted, average 12 Ibs. 31 rod licences; no returns made.

1884. 20,000 netted; 44 rod licences; no returns made. In this year Mr. Willis Bund, the Chairman of the Board of

VOL. I.

Conservators, published his very interesting book of *Salmon Problems.*

1885. 20,000 netted. 45 rods caught 40 salmon.

1886. 20,500 netted; 33 rods caught 60 salmon, average 12 Ibs. The Worcester sewage and some minor pollutions abolished.

1887. 27,000 netted ; 33 rods caught 20 salmon.

1888. 29,475 netted; a catch which placed the Severn in the rank of the most productive river in England ; 24 rods caught 24 salmon.

1889. 17,950 netted, 13 Ibs. average; 23 rods caught 50 salmon of 15 Ibs. average.

1890. 13,450 netted; 25 rods caught 50 salmon.

1891. 27,000 netted, 12 Ibs. average; 34 rods caught 200 salmon.

1892. 25,000 netted, 13 Ibs. average; 44 rods caught 150 salmon.

1893. 14,000 netted; 43 rods caught 50 salmon.

1894. 11,400 netted; 50 rods caught about 100 salmon.

1895. 12,900 netted; 40 rods caught about 100 salmon.

1896. 17,850 netted, average 13 Ibs. ; 37 rods caught about 150 salmon.

1897. 14,900 netted, average 13 Ibs. ; 32 rods caught about 100 salmon.

1898. 8,500 netted, average 13 Ibs.; 37 rods caught about 50 salmon.

1899. 10,000 netted, average 12 Ibs.; 27 rods caught about 50 salmon.

1900. 10,475 netted, average 12 Ibs; 14 rods caught about 25 salmon.

1901. 17,975 netted; 15 rods caught about 25 salmon.

1902. 20,950 netted; 18 rod licencees at *los.* caught 50 fish ; 5,479 trout licences, some at *2s.,* some at *is.*

From the above returns it may be seen that in the twenty years from 1882 to 1901 the Severn yielded 363,825 salmon to the nets, an average of very nearly 18,200 fish per season. In the same twenty years it yielded but 1,390 fish to the rod, or an average of 68 fish a season ; in arriving at these figures the rod catch for those seasons for which no returns were made has been estimated as if it had been the same as the last recorded season; in all probability it would not have been greater or the fact would have been mentioned, and most likely it was considerably less. Also it must be borne in mind that from 1891, when the largest reported take of 200 salmon was made, the rod catches of that and all the following years are reported as being "about" such and such a number ; this means that they were under the number named, and so consequently the estimate that 1,390 fish were caught by rods in these twenty years is considerably in excess of what really were captured. However, letting the figures stand as they are, it is bad enough in all conscience, for they show 261 fish to the net for each one to the rod, which is by far the heaviest percentage in favour of the net as against the rod of any river in the United Kingdom.

A gentleman who has known the Severn for the past thirty years writes me as follows :|"As to the salmon fishing on the upper Severn I do not think the river can be called a salmon angling river at all; it is true that a certain amount of fish get up to breed, and occasionally I have known that a few fish have been taken by the rod at Newtown, but not of late years. For nearly forty years I have fished for salmon in the Verniew and Its tributary the Banwy, and about thirty years ago I used to take a few fish each year; my largest catch in any one season was nineteen, though in the past ten years I have only caught five fish, all in October. Formerly I used to get a few fish in the spring and summer, but now they are entirely October fish ; in fact there is now no run of fish until the nets are off in September. At that time the rod season used to be from February ist to ist November, but a bye-law has lately been passed which closes the rod fishing at the 2nd October, which deprivesthe anglers of the best chance they had, poor even as it was."

There can be no doubt that the netting carried on in so many miles of the river entirely prevents the fish from reaching the upper waters until the close of the rod season. There is a public right of netting up to Tewkesbury Weir, and wherever similar public rights have been exercised they have never failed to ruin the waters above them. It is generally considered that there is no public right above Tewkesbury Weir, though there are a few who maintain this extends as far as Worcester, to which city they allege that the tide flowed before the weirs were made. Above Worcester private nets are used in various parts of the river up to Lincombe Weir near Stourport, which is getting on for fifty miles above the estuary. Therefore, until this netting can be done away with, the proprietors of the Severn above Stourport must abandon all hope of seeing salmon in their waters in any numbers worthy of mention. Nets work from February ist to 3ist August; rod season from February ist to 2nd October; salmon rod licence, *Ids.* ; trout rod licence in Salop, Montgomery and Denbigh, *2s.* ; trout rod licence in rest of district, *is.*

Chairman of Board of Conservators: Mr. I. W. Willis Bund, 15, Old Square, Lincoln's Inn Fields. *Clerk:* Mr. J. Stallard Jun., Pierpoint Street, Worcester.

14

SECTION 14

Chapter XIV
THE WYE

The Wye rises close to the Severn in the desolate bogs and morasses of Plinlimmon, where, in the days of King Henry IV., that turbulent Prince Owen Glendower, of Shakes- perian fame, made his stronghold. Some ten miles below the source of the Wye is the village of Llangurig, the first small assemblage of houses and trees to appear on its banks: from there it flows rapidly over a rocky bed to Rhayader, a little below which it divides the Counties of Radnorshire and Breconshire until it enters Herefordshire at Hay. About ten miles beyond Rhayader the large tributary of the Ithon falls in on the north, with the famous health resort of Llandrindod Wells on its banks. At Builth the Wye is joined by another large tributary on the right bank, the Irthon. Both these tributaries yield good salmon angling, especially in the autumn, but earlier if there has been plenty of rain. On August 28th, 1903, Mr. C. W. Woosnam took a fish of 35 Ibs. from the Irthon, the largest caught for many years,J

I

-I

D ffl

though one of 45 Ibs. taken about twenty years ago is still the record fish of the Irthon. But to return to the Wye, which now winds its way past Aberedw, Llandilo, Llanstephan, Boughrood, Glasbury, Maeswllch Castle and Clyro Court till it reaches the ancient town of Hay, from whence it continues its way past the ruins of Clifford Castle, the birthplace of Fair Rosamond, and it is strange that the anglers of these parts have neglected to call some specially pretty salmon fly after the ill-fated beauty of Woodstock; then come Whitney Court, Letton Court and Moccos Court until Hereford is reached, the birthplace of another famous beauty, Nell Gwynne, and here, as in many other places, it was once the custom to insert a clause in the indentures of apprentices that they were not to be fed on salmon more than two days in each week: would that the same clause was still a necessity!

Below Hereford comes Rotherwas, Mordiford, where the large tributary of the Lugg enters, Holme Lacy, Fownhope, Bolstone, Aramstone, King's Capel and Ross; between Hereford and Ross the Wye flows in a broad widening stream, many parts of its banks hereabouts being associated with the good deeds of John Kyrle, the famous " Man of Ross." Below Ross come the estates of Bishops Wood, Goodrich, and Welsh Bicknor ; then, winding its way by thetourist-haunted Symonds Yat, the Wye arrives at Monmouth, to be joined by the Monnow, and from here it sweeps in broad and graceful curves to join the estuary of the Severn. The whole river is from 140 to 150 miles in length, and drains 1,655 square miles.

From the source to Llangurig is about ... ... n miles.
Llangurig to Rhayader , n
Rhayader to Builth 16
,, Builth to Glasbury 20
,, Glasbury to Hay 6
Hay to Whitney 5
Whitney to Hereford ... ... 22 ,,
Hereford to Ross 25
Ross to Monmouth ... ... 15 ,,
, Monmouth to the Sea ,, ... 16

The Wye hardly suffers from any serious pollution, though there are mines on some of the tributaries, while it is singularly free from weir obstruction, as there are none between Chepstow and Rhayader, a distance of over 100 miles.

In 1860 the Wye salmon fisheries were at a very low ebb, for the tideway and all the lower part of the river was over-netted, while the kelts were incessantly poached in the upper reaches: as to the parr and the smolts, it was estimated that fully 200 anglers fished regularly for fry between Monmouth and Hereford, each taking from 100 to 150 a day in the season, and at that period the hotels of the neighbourhood were filled with visitors, who came for the express purpose of eating " Wye whitebait." Indeed, at this date had the Wye been subject to the same obstructions, pollutions, and wholesale netting as the Severn, it would have been pretty well wiped out as a salmon water; thanks, however, to the absence of these evils, the river kept comparatively well stocked.

In 1862 the late Duke of Beaufort, who then owned the lower fisheries, contributed .$300 towards the better protection of the river, while the upper proprietors, not to be outdone, clubbed together, and made up a similar sum : this resulted in the employment of some forty bailiffs, who acted so vigorously that poaching was no longer the easy, matter-of- course, profitable amusement that it had been : so loud and violent were the threats of the poachers, that fears were entertained that their repression would lead to bloodshed; but when it came to actual business, the poachers|to their credit be it said|wisely recognized that they would ultimately be beaten, and not one single case of assault occurred.

In 1863 a considerable improvement was reported throughout all the upper reaches as to the number of fish seen on the spawning beds.

1864. This increase of fish was at once met by a great increase in the putts, putchers, and nets of the estuary, so much so, that the upper proprietors objected to paying for the preservation of salmon nearly all of which were caught by the estuary nets.

1865. A Board of Conservators was formed, and licences issued for nets and rods.

The first clean fish are usually taken in March, though the main harvest is in June and July: grilse run in June and July; kelts are gone by the ist of May ; spawning is done in December.

1867. 169 rod licences issued at 205.

1868. There was a great decrease in the number of botchers or grilse, while there was a general feeling amongst the upper proprietors that the Act of 1861 had not tended to increase the stock of fish in their waters as it had been meant to do.

118 rod licences at 2O.r. ; no return of nettings or rod takes procurable.

1869. 112 rod licences. No return of nets or rods procurable. Arrangements were made with the Directors of a lead mine near the source of the river, by which its pollution was for the future to be run into settling tanks. Attempts were made to place fish passes on the weirs of the Monnow.

1870. 81 rod licences.

1871. 106 rod licences.

1872. 154 rod licences. Attempts were made to abolish night netting in the river.

1873. 165 rod licences.

1874. 154 rod licences. There was a very marked decrease of salmon, grilse, kelts, smolts and fry, a most unsatisfactory result after the river had been protected for twelve years under the new Fishery Laws of 1861. The severe netting in the river itself was doubtlessly the chief cause of this decline.

1875. 149 rod licences.

1876. The Conservators stated that they were unable to give any return of the number of fish netted, as the lessees of the nettings declined to give any information. It was estimated that in 1874 about 12,000 fish were netted; 145 rod licences.

1877. 150 rod licences.

1878. In this year 84 nets and 1,747 putchers were at work, while the lawless poaching of fish from the spawning beds was more openly and defiantly carried on than at any previous time; 139 rod licences.

1879. 114 rod licences.

1880. 123 rod licences.

1881. 129 rod licences.

1882. 130 rod licences.

1883. 140 at *2os.*, 26 at io.y.; some disease appeared.

1884. 152 at *2os.*, 19 at Io.t. ; a very dry season.

1885. 175 at 205., 20 at *Iqs.*

1886. 173 at *2os.*, 19 at iOi'.

1887. 163 at *2os.*, 6 at *los.;* a very dry season. The Hereford sewage was diverted from falling direct into the river.

1888. 182 at *2os.*, 31 at 105-.

1889. 203 at *2os.*, 24 at los. ; 2299 trout licences at *is.* The *Iqs.* salmon licence was for anglers fishing entirely above Builth.

1890. 154 at *2os.*, 25 at *i os.*

1891. 186 at *2os.*, 42 at 10.?.

1892. 153 at *2os.*, 44 at *los.*

1893. 154 at *2os.*, 33 at *los.* ; there was a great deal of disease, and the salmon yield all round was very much below the average.

1894. T57 at 2OS-i 29 at los-

x95- J3T at 2OS- JS at *los.* ; a very bad season all round.

1896. 144 at 205., 17 at *los.* ; many fish were found dead in the sluggish pools between Hereford and Ross, which were supposed to have been killed by pollution.

1897. 154 at *2os.*, 18 at *los.* ; again a very bad season.

1898. 181 at *2os.*, ii at *los.* ; a very poor season.

1899. 126 at *2os.*, 10 at *Iqs.* ; a very poor season.

1900. 114 at *2os.*, *12* at *Iqs.* ; the Conservators reported that in the last sixteen years there had only been one season which had been above the average, that two seasons had been average ones, and that the other thirteen seasons had all been below the average.

1901. Mr. C. E. Fryer, the Inspector of Fisheries, stated that up to this date the fresh waters of the Wye had been netted to a greater extent, and for a greater length, than any other river in England or Wales ; nets having been used at intervals all the way up to Whitney, which is about twenty miles above Hereford, and some ninety miles from the sea. That persistent and hard netting in fresh waters is deadly to the welfare of the salmon is a matter which is absolutely indisputable, for wherever it has been done in England, Wales, Scotland, or Ireland, it has ever resulted in disaster. Thus, year by year, the Wye fisheries declined, until at length the owners of nets in the lower waters, and the owners of anglings in the upper reaches, alike combined to make a common outcry. The owner of the Goodrich Court net fishing, which lies some thirty miles below Hereford, handedThis shows 963 salmon for the first five years, and but 351 for the five seasons following, and on account of the small returns of the last three seasons this net was not fished in 1901.

in thefollowing statement tothe Conservatorsshowing thetakesof his draughtnet since1891 :-| Salmon. Salmon. 1891366189674 18921 601897104 1893I IO189868 1894187189959 18951401 90046Another owner, whose fishery is situated about ten miles below the Goodrich Court net, stated he had known the Wye for thirty years, but had only used a net for the past seven years; that its yield was falling off, that while twenty years ago he used to catch six or seven fish in a day by rod, he never had " as much as a rise" in the season of 1900, and that he was now going to discontinue the use of his net for the good of the river. Another owner of a lengthy fishery a little above Hereford, stated that for the past ten seasons his rod catch had not averaged more than three fish per season. A Radnorshire proprietor who had never netted, stated that his fish book showed a large decrease not only in the number of salmon, but in the quantity ofgrilse, but that the average weight of the fish caught had increased from about 9-Ibs. in the period from 1860 to 1870, to 18 Ibs. in the period from 1890 to 1900; he now rarely saw a grilse, and for the last five years he had hardly seen a salmon in his waters. Another Radnorshire proprietor testified that, though he occasionally got a few fish in March and April, they had become fewer and fewer, and that he now caught no grilse at all, and that in wet seasons with plenty of water he now got fewer salmon than he formerly used to catch in dry seasons. 112 rod licences at *205.* ; 12 at *los.*

1902. In the previous year the net fishings lying between Hereford and Monmouth were leased by the Wye Fisheries Association, with the object of supplementing the legal regulations by abandoning the use of the nets ; there were eleven of these fisheries, each with a draught net, for which the Association paid ,$400 a year; a short time later on they formed a Committee for the express purpose of leasing from the Crown the fisheries which used to belong to the Duke of Beaufort; these extended from Monmouth to the sea, a distance of some twenty miles, in which were formerly worked some fifty nets with the right to erect more than 1,500 putchers. The Association has now leased the whole of them from the Crown for twenty-one years, at ,$525 per annum, subject to certain conditions, of which the most important isthat there shall be no net fishing above Chepstow Bridge, and none at all after the annual produce has realised ,$2,000, such sum to be applied to payment of rent, rates and taxes, water bailiffs' wages, and of a sum to the Conservators equivalent to the duty they would have received in respect of the engines now abolished ; and of a sum not exceeding 100 to the Wye Fisheries Association to go towards the leasing of the upper fisheries.

Therefore, as I write in this spring of 1903, there will practically be no netting to speak of from Hereford to Chepstow : there are in that distance a few proprietors who have not joined the Association scheme, but they are not many, and though, naturally, their few nets will get more fish than they formerly did get, they are neither sufficiently powerful nor numerous to stop the whole additional run of fish which will now be brought into the river by the abandoning of the many nets leased by the Association. Already, as I write, good accounts reach me of unwonted rod catches being made on the anglings between Whitney and Builth, and, under such altered circumstances, I can see no reason why the anglings of the Wye should not eventually become the best in England, for its pools are splendid to look at, while their occupants are of heavy weights and of the very best for the table. Between Llangurig and Builth there are many

-I *111*

excellent stretches of rapid running water: in this section the chief anglings are those of Llandrain, owner J. Rhys Pryse; Dderw, owner Revd. W. E. Pickard; Glanrh6s, owner L. J. Graham Clarke; Doldowlod, owner J. W. Gibson Watt ; Llysdinam, owner

C. Venables-Llewelyn; Brynwern, owner W. Clifton Mogg; Wellfield, owner E. D. Thomas; Caer Beris, owner Captain Harcourt Wood; Chapel House, owner W. T. Powell.

The Glanrh6s water extends down from Llanwrthwl Bridge for about three-quarters of a mile on the Breconshire bank, and with it is usually let the Upper Doldowlod water, which is on the Radnorshire bank and extends downwards for about the same distance : the whole is sometimes let with Glanrh6s House for a month or two ; in the upper water there are six good pools and five " bitties," all of which can be fished without wading. On the lower water there are four pools and three minor catches and wading stockings are necessary. With plenty of water, March, April and May are the best months for spring fish, July and August for grilse, with autumn fish coming from the middle of September to the end of the season on ist October. A rod of from sixteen to eighteen feet will be wanted throughout the whole of the Wye and no gaff may be used before 2nd April. Practically there are no sea trout in the river,though now and again one is taken. For heavy water a Britannia on a 2/0 hook is the best fly that can be used here, but all over the Wye Jock Scott, Silver Doctor, Thunder and Lightning, and indeed nearly the whole of the standard pattern, will kill; indeed these appear to have quite superseded the old native flies with their long hackles and strips of turkey wing. Spring fish average about 20 Ibs., grilse from 4 to 6 Ibs., but Mr. Graham Clarke, a right good fisherman with a thirty years' experience of the river, has caught them as small as 3 Ibs. and as heavy as 8 Ibs.

Some years ago he also caught six spring fish in one May day, which averaged 14 Ibs. Showery weather suits this water the best, but a stranger should keep a sharp look out for any indications of a sudden rise, for the river hereabouts has been known to "come" 14 feet perpendicular in four hours! From above Llanwrthwl Bridge the angling licence is 155., and below that it is 30., though for the benefit of visitors fortnightly licences are issued at *los.*

The Doldowlod angling extends from the Railway- Station of the same name down to the Bridge at Newbridge, a total length of about five miles, of which three miles is on both sides, with one-and-a-half miles on the Radnorshire or left bank, and half-a-mile on the Breconshire one. The upper waterlthe half-mile sectionlusually called the Doldowlod

'*ll*

MR. L. J. GRAHAM CLARKE.

Common Water, is let to Mr. Graham Clarke, of Glanrh6s, and is described with his own angling. It has fished fairly well in this season, 1903, having given up 13 fish in May. Commencing at the end of this water is the Tanhouse Pool, one side only; then, on both sides, come the Argoed and the Red Pool, both very good; the Wash Pool, fair ; the Cefn Coed Channels, good. One side only : The Ash Tree, very good ; Sand Pool, uncertain; Fish Pool, very good; Llyn Camin, good. By arrangement with the owner of the opposite bank, Mr. Llewelyn, of Llysdinam, these pools, which are all close together at Newbridge, are fished by the anglers of the two estates on alternate days, Llysdinam having both sides on Tuesdays, Thursdays, and Saturdays, while Doldowlod takes the other ones, an excellent arrangement for both parties, as very early rising, racing for pools, and such petty jealousies, are thereby done away with ; waders of some sort are indispensable ; for a tall man with long legs, stockings and an i8-ft. rod may suffice, though the majority of anglers will find a i6-ft. rod and trousers preferable. The water easily carries three rods, who here, as in other parts of the Wye, will find the Spey cast come in very handy : spring fish average about 20 Ibs., and flies of from size four Limerick down to size one are used. On May nth, 1903, Mr. W. B. Tylden Pattenson caught fish of , 16, and 14 Ibs., and lost another; on the i2th he hadtwo of 23 Ibs. each, the two days making a record for this water. These five fish were all caught on a fly which Mr. Pattenson made up, and which, as it lacked a name, he christened the " Doldowlod," on account of its success. A sombre, weird-looking, simple fly, the dressing of which is as follows :|

Tag: Silver tinsel.

Tail: Ibis.

Body: Grey badger fur, ribbed with silver tinsel.

Hackles: Badger fur picked out, with more tied in at shoulder.

Wings: Double strips of pea hen or grey Turkey wing ; strips of bustard over them.

Head: Black.

Mr. Graham Clarke informs me that, for the first time, bull trout have appeared in this spring of 1903, and, as these are not welcome visitors in a salmon river, it is to be hoped they will not increase.

The Brynwern Hall water at Newbridge extends for one-and-a-quarter miles on the right bank, the proprietor keeping in his own hands the five good pools it contains, all of which require wading trousers. The angling has much fallen off in the last ten years, and grilse have become almost unknown, and about eight spring fish of about 20 Ibs.is the average take at present. This section fishes best in fairly high water and keeps in good order for three or four days. Before the bad times set in Mr. Graham Clarke rented this water, and one day after the Lapstone and Llyngorse Pools had been hard fished by two friends all the morning with no result, he came down to them in the

THE FISH POOL.

afternoonl-it was Septemberland took eleven fish from them weighing 147 Ibs.

The Caer-Beris water commences at the Goitre Pool about two miles above the North Western Railway Bridge, and extends down on the right bank only, to within a quarter-of-a-mile of the bridge. It is kept in the owner'shands, and holds ten good pools, most of which require wading trousers, the best of them being Goitre, Gallynon Stream and Pool, Plum Tree and Cabia: Durham Ranger, Childers, Silver Grey, Silver Doctor, Jock Scott, and Thunder and Lightning are here the favourite flies, but any lures are permitted all over the Wye, and thus natural minnow, gudgeon, prawn and worm each have their partisans. The last ten years have been so bad that the average take of spring fish has fallen away to about eight per season, though before the bad times commenced this fine stretch of water yielded some very much better sport. On the 23rd of May, 1894, Captain Harcourt Wood caught five salmon in the Gallynon's, all with Jock Scott, 31 Ibs., 27 Ibs., 2i$ Ibs., 18 Ibs., 152- Ibs. which shows the splendid average of 22- Ibs.

Between Builth and Hay lie the cream of the Wye anglings, for the river swelling in volume while maintaining its rapid course keeps the pools in order for many days, while as they become larger, deeper and wider they offer the fish all the shelter they could possibly desire. The chief anglings of this lengthy stretch of water are those of Chapel House, owner Mr. WT. T. Powell; Ponshony, owner Mr. J. B. Mynors; Erwood Hall, owner Mrs. McWilliam ; Gwernyfed Park, owner Mr. T. Wood ; Velinnewydd, owner Mr. T. W. Vaughan; Maeswllch Castle, owner CaptainWalter de Winton; Clyro Court, owner Mr. R. H. Basker- ville; Cabalva, owner Mr. A. E. Marsland.

The Velinnewydd or Skreen water extends for about one-and-a-half miles on the Radnorshire bank and lies above the Gwernyfod Park section. Until about three or four years ago it was always in the owner's hands, but it is now let with Skreen House. There are six good pools in the water of which Killia and Doythog are the best, and excepting for the last named all require wading trousers. The water carries two rods comfortably, and in addition to the standard patterns of flies, an old Wye pattern still does execution: tail red ibis, yellow mohair body, blue hackle, brown turkey wings, whiteish at the tips. Here also in quite low water the worm is killing. Up till the time the angling was let, the take was from ten to fifteen fish to end of May, and rather more than that in the autumn. Salmon average 15 Ibs. ; grilse, of which there are very few, 4 Ibs. On May 6th, 1882, Mr. T. W. Vaughan and Mr. A. Gwynne Vaughan killed 4 salmon averaging 12 Ibs., and previously to that, on April 22nd, 1878, Mr. T. W. Vaughan caught a spring fish of 24 Ibs., the heaviest ever taken from this section, which is distinctly a high water one, though fish may be killed in " Boat Cafan " until it becomes dead low.

We next come to the splendid twelve miles of theMaeswllch Castle water belonging to Capt. Walter de Winton, and in which is comprised the pick of the Wye anglings, for probably more fish are caught in it than on all the rest of the river combined. Commencing close to Aberedw Station about three-and-a-half miles below Builth Wells, the Tercellyn beat is let on lease to Mr. R. Lewis Lloyd ; then comes the famous Nyth water, the best bit of the whole Wye, and let

THE AGIN POOL IN LOW WATER.

for this spring of 1903 to Mr. Edward Miller Mundy ; and here Mr. W. Hartopp, in the first week of April, 1903, had four fish in one day from the Cafan Pool, a day of fine sport, as the weights were 32, 30, 20, and 15 Ibs. ; the summer and autumn angling is let to other tenants. The Nyth extends for about one-and-a-half miles on both banks and, though often let by the season, is never let on lease ; it contains asplendid series of fourteen fine rocky pools, two of which are boated, two are cast from planks, a very pleasant way of reaching the lie of the salmon so soon as the angler has acquired the knack of standing over deep, sharp-running water without feeling giddy, while the remainder are fished by wading; but inasmuch as the going is not of the best, as it is chiefly over rocks, some caution is required, especially if the water be at all dirty and the foothold invisible ; when this section is in good ply there is a real long day for any two of the most hard-working rods, and unless there are two "gluttons" on the Nyth there is plenty of room for a third rod.

There is a charmingly placed fishing bungalow built on the banks of the best pool, heather-clad moors and mountains rise behind it, so that the surrounding scenery is quite in accord with the best traditions of Scotch or Irish salmon fishings, and if an angler was taken blindfolded to the Nyth he would be puzzled to know, when his eyes were uncovered, in which of the three Kingdoms he was. The best of the Nyth Pools are James Catch, Cefn Shon, Lewis, Never-say- die, Agin, Jack Dunn, Fernant, The General's, (called after the late General Goodlake, V.C., an old friend of the writer's, and recognized by all as one of the best of sportsmen and good fellows), Pull-y-vadd, and Isaacson; the cream of theseason is from the middle of April to the end of June for spring fish, for grilse from middle of July to middle of September, with September for autumn fish. When there is plenty of water in February and March, a few fish may be taken in the opening month, with more in March which are usually heavy ones. Nearly all the standard patterns of flies will kill, while the old Welsh ones are not to be despised ; of baits, worm, prawn, and Phantom are the best in the order named. All the year round salmon average about 15 Ibs., and grilse from 6 to 7 Ibs., and though there are most fish killed when the water is on the high side, some of the pools keep in good ply in all height of water; owing to the rocky nature of the bed, double gut casts are generally used and a rod of 17 to 18 ft. will be wanted ; flies are rarely dressed on any hook over 4/0 in size, and nearly all fish are taken on 3/0 Limericks.

Captain de Winton's Llanstephan water, which is below the Nyth, is let on lease to Mr. Aston Talbot; then below that, on the Radnor bank, Mr. Christy has a mile of the Maeswllch Castle water, while he rents Llangoed House and the angling opposite on the Brecon bank from Lord Glanusk. Then follows the Boughrood and Adams Catch water; nearly as famous as the Nyth and better known as the Woodlands water, and let on lease to Mr. William Tayleur, a brother-

in

-1

-1

S

K

in-law of Captain de Winton; this fine piece of water is sometimes let for May and the following months, as Yeomanry duties and trips to British Columbia combine to take the lessee from home. This beat extends from the Chapel Catch above Boughrood some five or six miles by river above Maeswllch Castle, to the tail of Adam's Catch, so famous for its big fish, the last of the leviathans falling to the rod of Captain Bailey in 1902, 42 Ibs. In this fishery, which is all on the Radnorshire or left bank, there are ten fine pools, three of which are divided into upper, lower and middle casts, other three are boated, and the rest require wading trousers. Here also April, May, and June are the best months, the grilse or botchers as they are called on the Wye and the Usk, running in July, August and September. The Woodlands water will always carry two rods with ease, while when the river is at its best height there is room for a third and perhaps a fourth.

Jock Scott, Childers, Wilkinson, Dunt, Dusty Miller, Ackroyd, Nova Scotia and Blue Monkey are the favourites here, while in times of low water the worm is often deadly ; one great advantage possessed by this stretch of water is that it runs down very slowly and so remains in order for many days in succession. In this season of 1903 it was only in order for two days in February on account of the exceptionalrainfall, when on the 2Oth a salmon of 28 Ibs. was caught ; it was in flood the whole of March, when the only capture was a remarkable one ; a sea trout of 4 Ibs., a very rare event, as these fish are almost unknown on the Wye. April ist saw the capture of a 22-pounder, the 2nd one of 18l- Ibs., the 6th one of 18 Ibs., the yth three of 28, 24 and 21 Ibs., the 8th one of 21 Ibs., the nth one of 14 Ibs. and 13th one of 10 Ibs., all these ten falling to the rod of Mr. William Tayleur, the last one being somewhat of a contrast to one of 68 Ibs. taken by him on the 3rd September, 1899, from the Campbell River of British Columbia.

An unpleasant adventure, however, happened to Mr. Tayleur, when fishing in this season 1903 with Mr. Venables Llewelyn at Lysdinam. On the 3ist March he hooked a fish at the Junction Pool, where the Irwen comes in to discolour the main stream with its dirty waters ; up this small tributary the fish tried to run, and as the rod was on the opposite bank, it was a case of holding on. Eventually the fish was beaten and brought nearly to the net, a sunken ledge of rock preventing the ghillie from quite reaching it ; as the man had no waders on, and wanted to keep dry, several unavailing scoops were made at the fish, each one sending it out into the stream jiggering in a most dangerous manner, and the situation becoming critical, for an old handnearly always can feel that the hold on a fish is wearing out some minutes before the event actually occurs, Mr. Tayleur, remembering that it was but a few hours before the gaff could legally be used, handed to Mr. Llewelyn a small telescopic one from his bag, which had been put there in readiness for the morrow: at that moment the hook came away, and the fish lay, apparently dead, in the shallow water that flowed over the rock. Owing, however, to a strong ripple, Mr. Llewelyn could not quite make it out, so, laying his rod on the bank, Mr. Tayleur ran to get hold of the gaff, only to find the fish sinking into deep water as he neared it; a hasty snatch merely scratched it, and then, as it vanished, he made a deeper mow at it, overbalanced, and plumped head foremost into twenty feet of water, as he felt the fish kicking on the gaff; the angler was, however, more easily landed than the fish, which escaped. On the I5th April Mr. Llewelyn's keeper caught the same fish from the same pool on a prawn, the gaff markslone a scratch, the other very deepltestifying to its identity ; weight, 27 Ibs.

Below Woodlands comes the Park Gwynne and Sheds water, which also belongs to Captain de Winton, and is let with Park Gwynne House. This consists of about a mile of the river, on which there are two good catches. Following this comes the Maeswllch Castle water, which begins at

VOL. I.

Glasbury Bridge, and goes down to the Clyro March, a distance of some two miles. Now, as up to this season of 1903 the total extent of the Maeswllch water had been let as a whole, and as this lower part was not such tempting-looking water as that which was above Glasbury Bridge, it had been much neglected by the various lessees, though there are four fine long pools on it which will be certain to yield sport so soon as they are regularly fished ; for at Clyro, where the pools are similar in characterlthat is, not so rocky or so rapid as those above Glasburyla good few fish are caught every season, and in April, 1903, three heavy ones were taken in one day. Captain de Winton also rents nearly the whole of the Breconshire bank of the river, so long as it runs opposite to his lands, chiefly from Lord Glanusk, and thus he secures the right of both banks for his tenants, though, curiously, with the exception of the Nyth water, almost every pool fishes best from the Radnor bank.

At Hay and below come the anglings of Clyro Court, owner Mr. R. H. Baskerville; Cabalva, owner Mr. A. E. Marsland; Whitney Court, owner Mr. J. Hope ; Letton Court, owner Mr. T. Dew; Moccas Court, owner the Rev. Sir George H. Cornewall, Bt.; Garnons, owner Captain Sir John R. Geers Cotterell, Bt.; Belmont, owner Mr. F. R. Wegg Prosser ; this latter a short stretch of water let to the Wye

tr u

Lu Lu

Conservators, and not of much account for the rod, while a little below this section is Hereford.

The Moccas Court water is situated in the parishes of Bradwardine, Moccas and Monnington and covers about seven miles, four of which are on the right bank, then about two miles of both banks, followed by one mile of the left bank. The angling is kept in the proprietor's hands, and consists of 14 large pools, for most of which wading trousers are indispensable, while when the river is at its best from four to six rods can be working. Turner's Boat, Coxcomb, Monk's Hole, Deep Well, Starford and Scaur are perhaps the most renowned catches. April is the principal month, while grilse never take well in this part of the river. Mar Lodge, Jock Scott, Childers, Popham, and the old Wye patterns are the favourite flies here, and anglers who fish the Annan and other rivers of Dumfriesshire will find that the old Wye patterns, with their rough mohair bodies, long hackles with slips of brown turkey for wings, are very much like the flies that are used in the northern river. The best bait lures are the natural minnow and the worm. For the past ten years, so greatly has the salmon supply fallen off that the rod take for the whole of this stretch of water has come down to about three or four spring fish each season ; in April, 1901, four fish were caught in three days by Mr. GeoffreyCornewall and Mr. J. F. Ray, average 19 Ibs. ; in April, 1902, three fish were taken in as many days by Mr. Geoffrey Cornewall and Mr. W. F. Cornewall, which averaged 22 Ibs. This is a low water fishery and remains in good order for fully a week after a flood.

Between Hereford and Ross the chief anglings are those of Rotherwas, Hampton and Holme Lacey, both of the latter being owned by the Earl of Chesterfield.

The Fownhope Fishery is in the hands of Trustees represented by Messrs. Symonds & Sons, Solicitors, Hereford, and lower down are Mr. Wyndham Smith's Aramstone Anglings. In March, 1902, the Hampton and Holme Lacey water yielded good sport, as about 30 heavy fish were got in the month, nine of which were caught in one day by the Earl of Chesterfield. In April following one more rod had another good day of five fish, which weighed 102 Ibs. Lower down at Fownhope Mr. Paterson also had fair sport, chiefly by the aid of the Silver Devon and real gudgeon, while in the Crown water at Ross Mr. A. Hoare had a fish of 41 Ibs.

Between Ross and Monmouth are the anglings of Hill Court, Major L. J. Trafford ; Bishop's Wood, Trustees of the late Colonel H. B. McCalmont; Courtfield, Colonel Vaughan ; Goodrich Court, Mr. H. C. Moffatt; Welsh Bicknor, The Reverend F. J. Aldrich Blake.

The Hill Court water is about three miles of the left bank, which the proprietor keeps in his own hands; there are six pools all of which require waders, and though stockings will usually serve, wading trowsers are better. March and April are the best months for all these lower waters.

The Courtfield water runs on both banks for about two- and-a-half miles and afterwards on the left bank for a further two-and-a-half miles. It is kept in the owner's hands ; there are five pools and streams, some of which are very lengthy, the " Park" and the " Monument" being the two best ; when the water is in right order fish may be looked for from the opening day to the end of April. Jock Scott, Butcher, Silver Grey and Durham Ranger are the favourite flies here, and prawn and minnow are the best bait lures. In 1902 three fish were got in one day and four in another by one rod from one pool.

The Goodrich Court water is some three miles in length and extends from about Glewstone Boat to White- brook below Kerne Railway Bridge, where there is a good pool called the Rocks; higher up the Doghole and Vanstone are the two best ; they can be waded or boated. Though this water has been kept in the owner's hands it has been very little fished.

VOL. I.

It may be said in summing up the Wye that above Builth the river only keeps in order for about three days after a flood; that a i6-ft. rod will cover these pools, in which the fish appear to rise more freely than lower down the river.

From Builth to Hay a rod of 17 or 18 ft. is wanted, and there are more fish in this section than in any other portion of the river. From Hay to the estuary, with a few exceptions, the pools are mostly long, placid-flowing reaches of water. Below Hereford the river becomes still deeper and more sluggish, but many big fish are nevertheless killed on the fly.

Close time for nets from i6th August to ist February ; above Bigsweir Bridge from i6th August to May ist ; for rod from i6th October to February ist.

Chairman : Mr. J. Hotchkis, Pontarfran, Brecon. *Clerk:* Mr. R. J. Owen, Builth Wells.

15

SECTION 15

Chapter XV
THE USK

The high, bleak, desolate hills of the Black Mountains which lie on the borders
of Carmarthenshire and Breconshire have the honour of sending on its journey to the
sea, this|the most famous|of English salmon rivers. The Henwru, with the Hydfer,
and other small brooks soon combine to turn it into a respectable river as it reaches
Trecastle, some eight miles from its source; from there it winds its way through the
Forest of Brecon, a lonely track of country which, in the time of Edward III., was the
shelter place of many a band of outlawed and desperate robbers. Before it reaches
Llanspydded, some three miles above Brecon, it receives the waters of several other
streams, the largest of which is the Yseir, falling in at Aberyseir; here the Usk turns
to the south to pass through a finely wooded valley on its way to Brecon|" built as
in a pit" as it is described in old chronicles|here the river is joined by the Taree and
Honddhu, the main stream being spanned by a substantial|and beautiful old bridge
with seven buttressed arches; it then wends its way towards Crickhowell through a
valley of great beauty, and passing the Parks of Glanusk, Llangattock and Dan-y-,
it sweeps with a graceful curve by Ty Maur to reach Abergavenny in a further two

or three miles. From this town|which like unto Brecon is also hill-surrounded| the Usk glides with a rapid, sedate flow of some fourteen miles to Usk with its " Three Salmons" Hotel, so well known to the anglers of the Association waters; about eight miles further on it meets the tide at Newbridge, below which there lie two pools which have often yielded heavy fish to those who cared to try them when the tide was out, and who had no objection to floundering about in the mud of the slob banks left by the considerable rise and fall of the water. From the end of the lower of these pools the Usk flows muddily past ancient Caerleon until it reaches Newport, eventually to merge itself in the Bristol Channel after a course of seventy-seven miles, in which it drains 650 square miles. Prior to 1842 a fishing mill-weir at Trostrey, a few miles above Usk, was an absolute bar to the further ascent of fish ; then a few gentlemen of the neighbourhood put their heads together, and renting the Trostrey Fishery for about ,$30, they made such alterations on the weir as were necessary to let up the fish; then keeping a lengthy stretch

ce CO

in

of the river below the weir entirely for their own angling, they sub-let the netting of the lower pools. At this period the angling was confined entirely to residents in the district, whose numbers did not exceed a score, and the advent of strangers coming from afar expressly for salmon fishing was something quite unheard of.

In 1846 the Usk Angling Association was formed, and after a long struggle against the ravages of the nets and the poachers it was on the brink of dissolution in 1861, when the passing of The Act encouraged the members to persist; from this small beginning grew the United Usk Angling Association, which in 1862 had Lord Llanover as its Chairman and one hundred and twenty members paying *$10* each per annum. Here then, as in nearly every instance elsewhere, it was the anglers who had been the chief promoters and largest contributors towards every movement calculated to restore to the depleted rivers the former glories of their salmon plenty; thus, although the anglers freely admit that their efforts have been made mainly to secure their own sport, it certainly should not be overlooked that in so doing they have largely helped to restore to the country a natural source of much wealth, and a food supply which prior to the passing of the 1861 Act had become nearly a thing of the past.

In 1862 arrangements were commenced for the formation of a Board of Conservators, but it was not until 1865 that the Board was properly constituted and endowed with the power of levying licence duties.

In 1866 197 rod licences were issued at 20., while nearly 3,000 fish were caught all over the river, many of them beyond Brecon, while several anglers each took more than 100 fish to their own rods.

1867. 248 licences at 20. This season was not so good as the previous one. The nets took about 2,000 fish and the rods about half that number. The first clean fish were usually got about the beginning of April, the main run being in May and June; grilse came in July and August. The run of smolts to the sea was in April, while after the middle of May kelts were seldom seen.

1868. 148 licences at 20. ; 48 at *Ids.* ; a very dry season, and angling was poor accordingly. Arrangements were completed for the purchase of Trostrey Weir by the

Conservators, with a view to its demolition; also some of the tributaries were opened up, and for the first time there cropped up that vexed question which still remains undecided, viz., the right of the Brecon Canal Company to extract an unlimited amount of water from the Usk.

1869. 177 rod licences at *2os.* It was again a very drysummer and consequently sport was poor, but it was noticed that there was a considerable increase of bull trout "to the detriment of the salmon." Trostrey Weir was destroyed, while the Forge Weir, which was now the nearest one above the tideway, offered very slight obstruction to the passage of fish. It was suggested by Mr. Walpole, the Fishery Inspector at this period, that the lower pools of the Association water should be netted in July and August; later on the proposal was carried into effect, greatly to the disgust and dismay of the upper proprietors, and to the astonishment of many of the anglers who were members of the Association, myself amongst the number. The evil still exists and will be alluded to again farther on.

1870. 133 licences at *2os.;* a very poor angling season.

1871. 191 licences at *2OS.;* the rods caught about *800* fish.

1872. 180 licences at *205.;* a good season. The nets took about 3,000 fish, and the rods caught upwards of 2,000.

1873. 177 licences at 20.; the nets got about 7,000 fish ; just over 2,000 fish fell to the rods.

1874. 196 licences at 205.; a poor angling season; the rods caught about 700 fish averaging 9 Ibs.

1875. 208 licences at *2os. ;* a "fairly good" season, which on any other river would have been described as a"splendid one," as the rods caught 1,129 fish averaging 9 Ibs.

1876. 171 licences at *2os. ;* a dry season ; the rods caught 566 fish.

1877. 213 licences at 20.; a good season with plenty of water ; the rods caught 1,537 fis weighing 14,850 Ibs., an average of 9 Ibs.

1878. 225 licences at 2Ctf.; the rods caught 1,241 fish. At this period Mr. A. D. Berrington, of Pant-y-goitre, was Chairman of the Board, with Colonel Lyne, of Newport, Secretary to the Association.

1879. 243 licences at 2cw.; trout licences issued for the first time, 1,746 at *is.* each. This was the best season ever known, as the rods caught about 3,500 fish averaging 10 Ibs. At this period the nets ceased on September ist, and began again on April ist; the rods ceased ist November, and started again with the nets.

1880. 250 licences at 2OJ. ; 1,986 trout at *is.* The rods caught 1,267 fis

1881. 240 licences at 20$. ; the rods caught 1,702 fish.

1882. 271 licences at 20$. The rods caught, mostly before the end of September, 2,452 fish averaging lOg- Ibs.; in the last twelve seasons 19,034 fish, or an average of 1,586 fish per season, have been caught by an average of 250 rods each
    season ; from 1846 to 1860 there were not twenty anglers using the river.

1883. 265 licences at *205. ;* 2,020 trout licences at *is.* The rods caught just over 2,000 fish averaging 10 Ibs. Salmon disease very bad.

1884. 202 licences at 2O.T. The rods caught 825 fish averaging 8 Ibs.

1885. 225 licences at *2os.* The rods caught 1,759 fish averaging 12 Ibs.

1886. 259 licences at 20. The rods got 1,658 fish, weighing 14,670 Ibs.

1887. 166 licences at 2oy. This was a very poor season and only 503 fish of 9 Ibs. average were caught. Complaints were made that from some of the tributaries, pollutions from collieries, iron mines, tin plate, chemical, naphtha and tan works were brought into the main stream, much to its injury.

1888. 266 licences at 20. No report issued. Disease very bad.

1889. 232 licences at 20. ; 2,150 trout licences at *is.* The rods caught 1,431 fish with a mean weight of 10 Ibs.

1890. 215 licences at 203. No returns.

1891. 323 licences at *2os.* The rods caught 4,931 fish averaging 10 Ibs.

1892. 305 licences at *2os.* No reports made. Salmon disease very bad in the early part of the year.

1893. 2I2 licences at 20. No returns made. Disease still very bad.

1894. 34 licences at 2CW. No returns made.

1895. 265 licences at 205. ; 2,114 trout licences at 15. The rods caught 1,362 fish averaging 10 Ibs.

1896. 229 licences at 2cxr. The rods caught 843 fish, 10 Ibs. average.

1897. 251 licences at *zos.* The rods caught 1,119 fish of 10 Ibs. average.

1898. 208 licences at *2os.* The rods caught 518 fish, average 12 Ibs.; very dry summer and autumn.

1899. 165 licences at *2os.* The rods only got 365 fish; again a very dry season.

1900. 197 licences at 20.?. 766 fish were caught, average 10 Ibs.

1901. 137 licences at *2os.* Only 198 fish, 12 Ibs. average, were caught.

1902. 125 licences at 20.; caught 741 salmon, weighing 6,647 Ids-

1903. The rods have caught just about 2,000 fish.

The United Usk Fishery Association have by degrees acquired many miles of the river, and, commencing on theright bank at the Llanover Brook, some three miles below Abergavenny, and on the left one at the bottom of the Brynderwyn Fishery, they extend (with the exception of two or three fields in two places) down to Redland Pool but a little above Caerleonlupwards of twenty miles of every variety of water divided into upper and lower fisheries, all particulars of which may be gathered from the following :I

1903.

RULES OF THE UNITED USK FISHERY ASSOCIATION.

Constituted for the purpose of assisting the Usk & Ebbw Board Of Conservators *in the preservation of their district.*

A. D. Berrington, Pant-y-goitre, near Abergavenny, *Chairman.*
Horace S. Lyne, Westgate Chambers, Newport, Mon., *Secretary.*

*(a)*lThe permanent Committee (hereinafter referred to as
" fVv
Committee.
"the Committee") shall consist of all members of the Usk

and Ebbw Board of Conservators; all ex-members of such Board appointed or qualified previous to November 5th, 1889; all owners and occupiers of Salmon Fisheries within the Usk and Ebbw Fishery District, qualified to act as ex-officio Conservators of such Board, or for any special reason appointed annually by the Committee: and one representative (to be elected annually) of the Class B Season Ticket-holders; in each of such cases being members of the Association, and having paid their subscription for the current year.

(l)|The Committee shall meet at such times and places
Powers of Committee!? Notices as they may determine, and act in such manner as they may *of Icetintrs*
deem fit for the making of the Rules and the management of the Association, subject to any objections by the Trustees of the Fisheries. If at any time the majority of the Trustees of any lease require a new Rule
or Rules to be made, or a then existing Rule or Rules to be repealed in respect of the Fishery with which they are concerned, such Rule or Rules
shall be made, repealed, or altered as the Trustees may require. The Chairman or any three members of the Committee, may direct the Secretary to call a Special Meeting of the Committee, and the Secretary shall give at least seven days' notice thereof, stating the objects of the meeting, and no other business than that specified in the notice shall be discussed at the meeting.

Subscription! (f)|No member shall be entitled to take part in any
to e pai meeting until his subscription shall have been paid. Annual
before acting.
subscribers of -$2 and under -$5 shall be entitled to one *Votes of Subscribers.* vote, and of .$5 and upwards to two votes. The Chairman shall have the customary casting vote.

Balance and (&)|After paying the rents, water-bailiff's and other e.-
Fvnd may be pggg of tne Association, the balance (if any), or any portion
paid to the Board r
of Conservators, of it may, in the discretion of the Committee, at the end of each year be handed over to the Board of Conservators, to be used by them in such manner as they may deem most expedient for the protection and improvement of the district.

(i?)|All Subscribers of *$2* and upwards per annum to
Subscriptions of
Members of the the General Fund of the Fishery District, approved by the Committee, shall become members of the Association. All subscriptions become payable to Mr. Horace S. Lyne, VVestgate Chambers, Newport, Mon., on the ist January in each year. Donors of ten times the amount of the annual subscription, approved by the Committee, may become Life members, with all the privileges of annual subscribers of one-tenth the amount of the donation. No member shall have any personal claim on the property of the Association, which is to be held by the Committee for the general benefit of the Fishery District.

(l)|A general meeting of the Association shall be held
"""a at least once in each year|not less than seven days' notice *Meeting.*

to be given of such meeting. At such meeting the accountsfor the past year, duly audited, shall be produced and circulated, and suggestions for the consideration of the Committee relating to the issue of Class B season tickets, or to the Rules of Angling in the Monmouthshire District may be discussed, if notice of them has been given to the Secretary at least ten days before the meeting, and inserted in the circular convening the same. Members who cannot attend may express their opinion on these suggestions by letter addressed to the Chairman not more than one month previous to the meeting, provided Rule *(c)* has been complied with, and such letters shall be laid before the meeting.

(g)|The Chairman, or any three members of the Com-
.' mittee, may instruct the Secretary to call a Special General
Meeting of the members of the Association, and the Secretary
shall state in the summons the nature of the business to be transacted at
such meeting, and give at least seven days' notice thereof, and no other
business than that stated in the notice shall be discussed at that meeting.

All Salmon Licences issued by the Board of Conservators can be obtained of Messrs. Mullock & Sons, Stationers, Austin Friars, Newport.

Salmon Rod Licences can be obtained of Mr. Evan Davies, *"oUaibu"* Post Office' Senny Brid8e of Mrs- Hughes, Stationer, Brecon; at the Railway Station, Talybont; of Mrs. Edwards, " Red Lion " Hotel, Llangynidr; of Mr. R. Harris, Chemist, Crickhowell; of Mr. D. T. Lewis, " Bell" Hotel, Llangrwyney; of Mr. C. J. Fricker, Stationer, Aber- gavenny; at the Post Office, Llanfihangel-Gobion; of Mrs. Creese, Post Office, Usk ; at the Post Office, Gilwern ; at the " Newbridge " Hotel, Newbridge; at the "Bridge" Inn, Chain Bridge; and at the "Angel" Hotel, Abergavenny (by visitors staying at the Hotel), on payment of $ for the season. A licence for fishing for Salmon covers fishing for Trout with the same description of instrument. Trout Rod Licences, for the Season, costing One Shilling each, may be procured of Mr. Watkins, Postmaster, Trecastle; Mr. Evan Davies, Post Office, Senny Bridge; Mrs. Hughes, Stationer, Brecon; The Station Master, Talybont; Mrs. Edwards, " Red Lion" Hotel, Llangynidr; Mr. R. Harris, Chemist, Crickhowell; Mr. D. T. Lewis, " Bell" Hotel, Llangroyney; Mr.

VOL. I. N

C. J. Fricker, Stationer, Abergavenny; The Station Master, Penpergwm ; Mrs. James, Postmistress, Llanfihangel-Gobion; the " Bridge" Inn, Chain Bridge ; Mrs. Creese, Post Office, Usk; Mr. Fox, Hairdresser, Pontypool; at the " Newbridge " Hotel, Newbridge ; Messrs. Mullock & Sons, Stationers, Newport; Mr. H. Edwards, Commercial Street, Newport; J. Young & Son, Chemists, Newport; Mrs. Jones, Post Office, Raglan ; at the Post Office, Gilwern; at the "Angel" Hotel, Abergavenny (by visitors staying at the Hotel); and of the Postmaster, Crumlin. Licences for Trout fishing with other instruments can be procured of Messrs. Mullock & Sons, Stationers, Newport; Supt. Vaughan Powell, Senny Bridge, Brecon; and Supt. M. Williams, Llanfair, near Pant-y-Goitre, Abergavenny.

Rules Under Which Tickets May Be Issued For The Monmouthshire District.

Subject to the Applicants being approved by the Committee.
i.|The Association Fisheries are divided into the Upper
InH 1
Fisheries.
and Lower Waters. The Upper Water consists of the Association
Fisheries from the mouth of the Llanover Brook downwards to the upper boundary of the Lan Fishery; including, speaking generally, the Pant-y-Goitre Fishery, and part of the Kemeys Fishery, but excluding the Llanvair Glebe and Pant Fisheries. The Lower Water consists of the Association Fisheries between the lower boundary of the Upper Water and Redland Pool, but does not include the Lan Fishery. The Clytha, Forge Mill, Brynderwen, Lan, and some other smaller Fisheries are not at present in the occupation of the Association. The fishing from off Trostrey Weir is exclusively reserved for Classes A, B, C. The Committee reserve the right
of netting.
2.|Mr. Hanbury reserves the right of angling for himself
Reservation of
Mr. Hanhtry's personally, and the right of giving previous notice to reserve
for any day the exclusive right of angling for salmon on any
one of the continuous Catches of the Crown Fishery, as they are numberedfrom 61 to 97, both inclusive, on the Card of Catches, for himself and friend staying at Pontypool Park ; also three tickets for the Crown Fishery, transferable by himself to his friends, but not transferable by them, but which are subject to the Rules of the Association and to the beat system. *Marquis of* The Marquis of Bute reserves certain rights of fishing on
B"'e- the Monkswood Fishery.
3.| All applications for Rules of the Association or for Salmon.
Season Salmon Season Tickets, whether for Salmon or Trout (except those under Rule 8), must be made to the Secretary, Mr. Horace S. Lyne, Westgate Chambers, Newport, Mon., who will only issue the tickets on payment of the price of each.
4. | The Committee reserve the right to issue two trans-
Class A.
ferable Salmon Season Tickets (Class A) at present held by Lord Tredegar and Mr. Berrington, and also to issue other similar tickets by way of arrangement with landowners and others. A transferable ticket can only be transferred by the owner or his recognised agent, and not by any person to whom he may have lent it, or for any pecuniary consideration. These tickets are issued subject to the Rules of the Association, and as regards the Lower Water, subject to the beat system. The Committee also reserve the right to issue free Trout Tickets to brinkers and free Dace Tickets.
5. | Sixteen non-transferable Season Salmon Tickets, at
Class /!.
each for the Lower Water, and twelve non-transferable Season Salmon Tickets at $26 each for the Upper Water, will be issued to members of the Association. Class B tickets on the Lower Water will be subject to the beat system.

6. I A list will be kept by the Secretary of all the appli- *"'f "* cants for Class B tickets, who are Members of the Association,

with the date of the receipt of the application. If any gentleman who has hitherto held a Class B ticket, or to whom one has been offered, neglects to apply for a fresh one before the first day of January in any season, and to pay for it before the loth day of February, it cannotbe reserved for him. A ticket once issued cannot be transferred to another name or exchanged; but if from any cause a ticket has not been issued, or has become no longer available, or is temporarily disused, the Secretary, with the approval of the Chairman, may issue a ticket of the same class in lieu thereof, either for a long or short period, and at such price and subject to such conditions as may be deemed advisable.

7.IThree non-transferable Salmon Day Tickets, Class C,

Salmon Day

Tickets, Class C, available on beats upper, middle, and lower, respectively, of 1 Creese, Usk Lid tne Lwer Water, and subject to the beat system, will be placed *Mrs./ames, Post* with Mrs Creese) Post office, Usk; the post office at Usk is

Office, Llanji'

hangel-Gobioti. open from 7 a.m. to 8 p.m. on week-days only. A book is to be kept on the counter, open to the inspection of all comers, and any person may claim to have his name entered in such book as engaging one of such tickets for any day or days not already occupied, *on payment of the price of the tickets, and not otherwise.* Provided that no person can engage tickets for more than three consecutive days before five o'clock in the evening of the last of such days ; and no person can engage a ticket for more than twenty-one days before the day for which it is required. The distributor must enter in the book the names of all persons who engage to take tickets, and will be answerable for the price of the ticket for every name entered in addition to any other ticket he may sell. The price for Class C tickets will be 2 os. per day. One similar ticket, available on the Upper Fishery, will be placed with Mrs. James, Post Office, Llanfihangel-Gobion.

8.ITickets (Class D) may be granted to angle for Salmon *Class D, Season* between the top of the Withy Bed (Catch No. 42) below

Tickets for

Salmon at ios., Trostrey and the County Bridge at Usk (the field belonging *limited Water* to "o McDonnell and any private gardens excepted) at 20. for the season to *land, fide* residents in the Usk and Ebbw Fishery District, within the County of Monmouth, and for Trout, between the Stable of the Old Mill at Trostrey and Pont Sampit (with the same exceptions), at 5. for the season. Such tickets can be obtained of Mrs. Creese, Usk; and of Mr. Fox, Hairdresser, Pontypool.

9.IAll salmon tickets include the right of angling for other fish during the trout season, subject to these rules.

may be itsea.

The regulations of the beat system are printed separately. They apply only to holders of Class A, B, and C Tickets, and do not apply to the Salmon Limited Water.

10.IExcept by special order of the Committee, no angling *ours of* js ajjowe(j before g a m. jn the event of two or more salmon

Angling.

anglers being at a Catch at 8 a.m. they shall draw lots for the first turn, unless one of them had the first fishing of that Catch on the previous fishing day, in which case he shall give way. No angling is allowed after 9 p.m. except during the months of June and July, when the hour is 10 p.m. All salmon tickets expire after the evening of November ist.

n.|The river is divided into different Catches, and *"cat-k' "'* t'le Keepers are provided with cards on which the name

of each Catch is printed. No angler will occupy a Catch while another is waiting to fish for more than half-an-hour: the time spent in playing a fish not to be counted. Anglers to take precedence in the order of their arrival. An angler may fish after another at not less than twenty-five yards distance without giving previous notice, when the man in front may only fish the Catch again by commencing behind all those who were following him. In the event of a fish being hooked, all other rods must give way. *(The question of the tu'enty-fire yards distance is reset red for the consideration of the Committee, and Rule 11 is therefore liable to some amendment).*

12.|The season for angling for Salmon commences on the 2nd March, and ends on the ist November, inclusive.

13.| All applications for Season Tickets and Rules of the

,.',,, Association must be made to the Secretary. Season Trout *Season Tickets.* !

Tickets will be issued at One Guinea each for the Upper Water, and One Guinea each for the Lower Water.

Season Trout 4-|Transferable Season Tickets, to be called House
House Tickets. Tickets, and available for angling for trout on both waters, may
VOL. I. N

be issued at 3 each to persons residing in the district, to be used only by the holder and one friend staying in his house, such friend not being resident in the County of Monmouth. If the applicant himself holds a season ticket, whether for salmon or trout angling, he may obtain a house ticket for use by one such friend for *$2,* or by two such friends for 3.

15.|Weekly and Daily Trout Tickets may be obtained of
Daily Trmtt Mrs- Creese, Post Office, Usk; of Messrs. Mullock & Sons,
Tickets. Newport; at the " Newbridge " Hotel, Newbridge; of Mr. C. J.
Fricker, Abergavenny; Mrs. James, Post Office, Llanfihangel-Gobion;
Mr. Fox, Hairdresser, Pontypool; the "Bridge" Inn, Chain Bridge; and the
Station Master, Penpergwm. For one trout rod, *zs. 6d.* per day, or
los. per week.

Trout Tickets on 16-|For Trout Tickets on the Limited Water (Class D),
Limited Waters. see Rule 8.

17.|Unless by special order of the Committee no angling *ours oj* .s aj]owe(j before g a-m or after p.m., except during the

months of June and July, when the hour is 10 p.m. 18.|All Trout Tickets include the right of angling, during the trout season, for other fish, except salmon (see Rule 33), subject to these rules. *Provision as to* 19.|That portion of a Salmon Catch occupied by a

Salmon Catches. Salmon ticket-holder shall not be fished by a Trout angler.

20.|Fishing for Trout, otherwise than with an artificial y, fr""/,",'" fly 's not allowed before ist June, except "bobbing," which is permitted from the ist May.

21.|All fish measuring less than six inches in length from

.Minimum , . r . . ., , ... , .

r i r- 7 the point of the nose to the fork of the tail are to be returned

Length of Fish.

to the water immediately after they are caught.

Licence required 22|Anglers using more than one rod at a time must *fo,-each rod used.* hold a licence for each rod.

Season for 23-|The season for angling for Trout commences on the

Trout. 2n(j Iarch and ends on the ist September inclusive.

Genf.ral Z4- | fis' l 'nS except fair rod and line angling, no

Prohibition of night line or night lobworm fishing, no fishing for Salmon

iodes of 'fishing. (except telow the bridge at Newbridge), except with an

artificial fly, and no spinning or bait fishing on Salmon Catches is allowed. The Committee may suspend this Rule, or any portion of it, in cases where the waters rented by the Association adjoin the waters of other fishery owners who may not agree to fish their waters in accordance with the Rules of the Association.

25. | No gaff shall be used as auxiliary to a rod and *Use of Gaff.* line, or had in possession on the river side by an angler or

his assistant before the ist May, or after the ist October,

and all persons fishing are required to supply themselves with landing nets in lieu thereof.

26. | A ticket-holder may not cut or lop any tree, sapling,

Prohibition of

the Cutting of bush, or weeds, in or near the river, or employ any person

Bushes, etc.

to do so. (See Rule 31. When any such act may be

deemed desirable it may only be done by a Water-bailiff or other person employed by the Association, under the direction of the Superintendent.)

27. | No ticket-holder on the Association waters is *No dogs allowed.* allowed to be accompanied by a dog.

2' | Sunday fishing is prohibited.

29. | Coracles must at all times be taken over the land *Use of Coracles,* past the Salmon Catches, except on the Salmon Limited Water

(Class D), or when used in connection with nets.

30. | Ticket-holders are required to obtain the licence of

Tickets and

Licences to be the Board of Conservators, and to show their tickets and *shovjii.*

licences when requested to do so. A Salmon Rod Licence

costs 205., and a Trout Rod Licence u.

31. | Any ticket-holder selling his fish, or lending his ticket, or acting contrary to these Rules, or violating any Act of Parliament for the preservation of fish, or any Bye-law of the Board of Conservators of the district, or conducting himself in

a manner unbecoming a gentleman, shallforfeit his ticket, and shall have no further claim on the Association or its Officers. In all cases of dispute, or of forfeiture of tickets, the decision of the Committee shall be final; and tickets are only issued subject to this condition.

32.|In the event of the holders of one-third of the total number of Salmon Season Tickets objecting in writing to the issue of a ticket under Class B to any person, the ticket shall not be granted to such person except by special resolution of the Committee.

33.|The Committee may decline to grant or renew any ticket to any person at their discretion. *Interpretation* 34.|The word " Salmon" in these Rules is to be

of the word

"Salmon." interpreted as in the Salmon Fishery Acts, 1861 to 1873.

Salmon Fishery Act, 1861, 24 And 25 Vic. Cap. 109, Sec. 4.

" *Salmon* " *shall include all migratory fish of the genus salmon, whether known by the names hereinafter mentioned, that is to say, salmon, cock or kipper, kelt, laurel, girling, grilse, botcher, blue cock, blue pole, fork tail, mart, peal, herring peal, may peal, pugg peal, harvest cock, sea trout, white trout, sewin, buntling, guiniad, tubs, yellow fin, sprod, herling, whiting, bull trout, whitling, scurf, burn tail, fry, samlet, smoult, smelt, skirling, or scarling, parr, spawn, pink, last spring, liepper, last brood, gravelling, shed, scad, blue fin, black tip, fingerling, brandling, brandling, or by any other local name.*

" *Young of Salmon" shall include all young of the salmon species, whether known by the names of fry, samlot, smolt, smelt, skirling, or skarling, par, spawn, pink, last spring, hepper, last brood, gravelling, shed, scad, blue fin, black tip, fingerling, brandling, brandling, or by any other name, local or othenvise.*

Holders of Trout Tickets and Trout Licences are prohibited from fishing for or taking any of the above Fish.

In the Brecon District the Association has again a considerable extent of angling. The Committee, their powers,rates of subscription, votes, annual and special meetings, and where licences are obtainable, are exactly the same as on the Monmouthshire water. The Rules for the issue of tickets are as follows :|

Rules Under Which Tickets May Be Issued For The Brecon District. *Subject to the applicants being approved by the Committee.*

i.|Tickets for angling in the waters of the Association between Aberbran Bridge and opposite the bottom of Defauden Meadow will be issued to all applicants, subject to the approval of the Committee, resident within one mile of the Town Hall, Brecon, at the following rates :| Salmon and Trout tickets for the season ... Iqj.

Trout tickets ... ... 5.

N.B.|The Pontarfran Meadow is not included in these waters. 2A.|Tickets for angling in any of the waters of the Association in Breconshire may be issued at the following rates :|These tickets will be forfeited if the holder sells any fish:|

Salmon and Trout tickets for the season ... 40.?.

,, for one week ... iof.

for one day ... 5.

2B.|Tickets for angling in any of the waters of the Association in Breconshire below Aberbran Bridge may be issued at the following rate. These tickets will be forfeited if the holder sells any fish :|

Salmon and Trout ticket for the season ... 20.

3.|All tickets and copies of the Rules may be obtained of Mrs. Hughes, Stationer, Brecon. Tickets under Rule 2A and copies of the Rules may also be obtained of the Secretary, Horace S. Lyne, Westgate Chambers, Newport, Mon. ; at the "Castle" Hotel, Brecon, by visitors staying at the Hotel; and Mr. Evan Davies, Post Office, Senny Bridge. Tickets are not available without the licence of the Board of Conservators. A Salmon Rod

Licence costs 205.; and a Trout Rod Licence, *is.*; a ticket once issued cannot be exchanged or returned.

4.|It is intended to grant free tickets to tenants approved by the Committee to angle for trout from land in their own occupation.

5.|All free tickets will be revocable at any time.

6.|The season for angling for Salmon commences on the 2nd of March and ends on the ist of November, inclusive.

7.|The season for angling for Trout commences on the 2nd of March and ends on the ist September, inclusive.

8.|No fishing, except fair rod and line, and no night line or night lobworm fishing is allowed.

9.|No fishing for trout, other than with an artificial fly, is allowed before the *i$th April.*

10.|Tickets for trout fishing are not available to holders of more than one Trout Licence.

ii.|No gaff shall be used as auxiliary'to rod and line, or had in possession on the river side by an angler or his assistant before the ist of May, or after the 3oth day of September in any year.

12. |No angling is allowed before 6 a.m., or after 9 p.m., except by special order of the Committee, and except in the months of June and July, when the hours shall be from 5 a.m. to 10 p.m.

13.|Ticket-holders are required to show their tickets and licences when requested to do so.

14.|Ticket-holders must be careful to ascertain the boundaries of the Association waters, as they are in certain places intersected by private fisheries.

15.|Any ticket-holder lending or transferring his ticket, or acting contrary to these Rules, or by himself or assistants violating any Act of Parliament for the preservation of fish, or assaulting any Keeper or Water- bailiff, shall thereby forfeit his ticket.

16.|If any objection should be raised to the forfeiture of a ticket, the matter shall be referred to the Committee, whose decision shall be final,u

W

O

E

O

UJ

iC

o

o

and until that decision is obtained the ticket shall not be available. In all cases of dispute the decision of the Committee shall be final.

17.|The Committee may decline to grant or renew any ticket to any person at their discretion.

18.|No ticket-holder on the Association waters is allowed to be accompanied by a dog.

19.|Sunday fishing is prohibited on the Association waters.

20.|The word " Salmon " in these Rules is to be interpreted as in the Salmon Fishery Acts, 1861 to 1873.

Both these Association waters are so excellently well worked that it is hardly possible to write too highly of their management. When first I became a member of the Lower Water Association|I think in about 1868|the yearly ticket was but .$15, while the cost of the daily ones, taken out from the Usk Post Office, was "js. 6d. In those days Sir Sandford Graham, Colonel Pipon, Mr. Morgan Vane, Mr. Carbonel, Colonel Legh, Mr. Thomas Lant and Colonel Rocke were usually to be found staying at the " Three Salmons," and of this select coterie of anglers I believe Colonel Legh is the only survivor. I think it was in 1869, or thereabouts, that Mr. Lant and I found ourselves at the Hotel during a July drought. Every pool swarmed with ceaselessly splashing fish, notably Pen Carreg, Rhyl-y-Derry and Coed-a-Prior; flies, minnows, natural and artificial, large prawns, and bunches of worms were in vain used by all the Members, until some ten days had elapsedwithout anyone making a single capture. Then, one evening, Lant hinted to me in a mysterious manner that, on the morrow, he hoped to have a lure that would prove a killer. The next morning I was first to attack the breakfast in the sitting-room we were sharing, and here a splendid dish of shrimps meeting

Mr. RICKARDS COMING TO COED-A-PRIOR.

my gaze, at them I went with a will ; presently in came my friend, whose face became as long as the top joint of his rod as his eyes rested reproachfully on the pile of heads and tails on my plate. " Good heavens," he cried, " why I wired for those shrimps to fish with, and not for us to eat." Then it turned out he had forgotten to tell his man to keep themin reserve, and so he had unpacked them and placed them ready for breakfast. I could not help laughing, as I answered, " Well! there is your half of 'em left ; and as I have eaten my share, I will come and watch you use them; but, really, you had better eat them, for they are deliciously fresh." But not one would he put to his lips, and, hurrying through his breakfast, the rest of the shrimps were transferred to a tin box, and we were soon on our way to the river. As I settled to halt at Pen

Carreg, Lant continued his way down stream, though, as we parted, he good-naturedly insisted on my giving the shrimps a trial, and forced a few on me, wrapped up in a piece of paper ; then he gave me a mounted hooklabout No. 4 Limerick sizelan ounce bullet with a hole drilled through it. " Fasten the lead on your line about a yard above the hook, then just thread the shrimp on the hook, and let the turn over of the tail cover the barb, then drop it in a few yards above any fish you see splash, and wait events," was his parting advice. So I did as I was instructed, and slipping the bait into the water above the first fish that moved, I laid the rod on the steep meadow bank (for I was on the right bank of the river) and drawing off a few yards of slack I mounted guard. Presently the line began to tremble and shake, and ultimately the slack began to pass quietly through the rings; then, seizing therod, I struck; there was not the faintest resistance, and up came a slimy, wriggling little eel, a long way under a pound in weight; thus, when this had happened several times, the little faith I had had in the shrimp as a salmon lure had entirely vanished, when the sight of a big fellow, which' I judged to be 25 Ibs., incited me to have another try. Fully a quarter- of-an-hour went by ere the line began to move with strong, quick tugs, followed by a rapid run out of the slack line, and this time, as I struck, I knew I was fast in a big fish.

The situation was somewhat unpleasant and cramped, as I had carelessly dropped in the bait between two tall poplar trees, which effectually prevented me from following my captive; stout tackle and a strong- rod eventually floated a splendid fish within reach of a gaff stroke made by the left hand while lying prone on the grassy bank above the water with head and shoulders protruded over it as far as was prudent ; then came many more eels, with three other good fish, by lunch time, when my supply of shrimps was exhausted ; so falling back on the useless fly, I fished a pool or two below, and seeing nothing of my friend, I worked back to the Hotel to find myself the first man home. Later on Lant was the last to appear with about a dozen salmonlI forget the exact number; of course all the others wanted to know with what lure our take had been made and Lant's discoverywas at once disclosed to them, which resulted in a stampede to the telegraph office and the ordering of quarts and quarts of shrimps. The next day Lant took, I think, seven other fish with the rest of his stock of bait. On the morning following shrimps arrived in goodly quantities and every one was provided, and I even had a few for breakfast; then, just as we had decided on what pools we would distribute ourselves, a wire arrived from the Committee of the Association to say that shrimp fishing had been prohibited at a meeting held the day previously ; of course there was nothing for it but to obey, and all did it with a good grace and without a growl, but when, a few days later, the Association bailiffs came and netted all the pools we certainly did think we should have been permitted to catch the salmon with shrimps instead of having to stand on the banks and watch them netted ! Of the proceeds of these hauls a few fish were given away to the farmers on the banks, though the bulk of them were sold for the benefit of the funds of the Association. I think I am correct in saying that from that time this fresh water netting by an Association existing avowedly for angling purposes only, has been continued in every succeeding season. Now, apart from any sentimental feeling as to the anomaly of an Angling Association turning itself into one that nets its fresh waterpools for profit, there also seems to me something not quite in accord with the spirit of the Association rule that strictly forbids the sale of rod-caught salmon ; for surely if it be considered wrong for the members of an Angling Association to sell their fish, how much more *infra dig.* must it appear to outsiders when the Committee order salmon to be netted and sold from the waters they profess to preserve purely for angling ? The proceeding puts out of joint and jars on all the preconceived ideas of fair play that exist so pronouncedly in the hearts of all good anglers.

Moreover the netting of these fish that have won what should be "the Sanctuary." after escaping all the perils of the estuary, also seems unfair to all the other Members of the Association who may fish the waters above where the netting takes place; especially is it hard on the riparian owners of the anglings that lie between the top of the Lower Association water and the bottom of the Breconshire one; in this distance are some of the best fisheries of the river, and it is a distinct hardship on their owners, that as the too frequent droughts of August come to an end, they should be robbed by these nets of the run of fish which the first September rains would have brought them from the accumulated salmon of the lower reaches ; any way this netting must inevitably rob the river of many breeding fish. It is possible there

NETTING THE BRYNDERWYN WATER.

A CONTRAST! ON THE FORGE STREAM.

may be some good reasons for these nettings, but if so I have never been able to ascertain them, and in my criticism of it I have many supporters who agree with me; it is certainly the only blot on the management of an Association whose rules have otherwise been worthy of copy wherever Angling Associations exist. On behalf of the fish and the already mentioned riparian owners this netting should certainly be discontinued; in the good times of 1879 perhaps this evil custom did not do any particular harm, for those were the days of fish-plenty, but as soon as a fish scarcity showed itself season after season, then surely, in the best interests of the fish and everyone concerned, it should have been discontinued. Personally, I think it would be a popular move in the right direction if the netting ceased, and the lower waters of the Association were thrown open to lures of all sorts during July and August, or for so long in these two months as the river was below a certain level. Nothing will ever convince me|in face of a lengthy experience|that the use of bait lures will spoil a river for the fly; selfish anglers who own or rent the best reaches of the best rivers|reaches abounding in pools in which the fish will lie for long periods, and in which, if they will not look at a fly one day, they will yet take it freely on the next| may often be heard to hurl anathemas on the heads of the

VOL. I.

bait fishers below them, while attributing a dour day entirely to the fact of the fish having seen a few prawns or minnows or worms on their way up stream !

In the language of Mrs. Gamp this is just " rubbidge"! It would be amusing to take some of these wealthy grumblers and transplant them on to some portion of their favourite river which was only a few miles above the tideway, and through which fish will run with hardly a halt ; on anglings of this sort the fly will be nearly, useless, though baits will often make a certain number of captures, but the rabid fly man tells the bait man with a lofty disdain of his lures, and with chest swelling with the importance of his own superior sportsmanlike qualities, that the bait fisher is simply a poacher, and that his landlord is but little better where he lets his angling without limiting it strictly to the fly only.

Well, if the landlords of the lower reaches of big rivers did that they would be sorely pressed to find tenants. While preferring to kill with the fly rather than by any other lure, I have over and over again tried the experiment, in anglings which have been situated but a few miles above the tideway, of fishing the feathers in front of a friend or a ghillie coming behind me later on with a bait lure ; in forty years never but once has the fly held its own in amonth's fishing. Then for a change I have reversed the proceedings, and except on the one occasion already alluded to, and which was a " dead heat," the take made by the bunch of feathers has never even approached my bait score. Then again, I will return to the picked fishings of a famous river, and I can only state that on the Glen Tana waters of the Dee, which is the very best angling of the very best river in the United Kingdom, and where I have spent many happy days, I have repeatedly killed fish with the fly from pools that I had seen only half-an-hour previously either minnowed, gudgeoned, phantomed, or prawned ; moreover, the late Sir William Cunliffe Brooks was of my way of thinking, and his visitors at Glen Tana were welcome to fish with any lure they fancied. I am neither a " rabid " fly man or a " raving" bait man, but I am most tolerant to every method of catching salmon so long as it be fairly done with rod and line, no matter the lure. But to return to the river : from Brecon and higher up there is not much spring fishing, unless one of the summer months has been very wet; if that has not been the case, then the first August or September flood takes the fish to Brecon and beyond. The Camden water, belonging to the Marquis Camden, is perhaps as far up as they ascend; it consists of about three miles of both sides, with half-a-dozen nice pools for which wading stockings arenecessary; below this on the right bank comes the Pentre- allog water belonging to Mr. Austin Powell, about one-and- a-quarter miles in length with eight good pools, of which the Clydach, the Governess, and the Coffin, are the best, and those which cannot be cast from the bank are easily commanded by wading stockings ; on this stretch Colonel Gough had four fish in a day, of a total weight of 60 Ibs. The opposite bank is fished by the Association ; below this comes the Ynnisllvyddfa section owned by Mr. Lloyd Downes. There is about two miles of both banks which is usually let ; the Chapel, Pot, Llewyn, and Farm Pools, are perhaps the best of the ten that are on this fishery, for which trousers are better than stockings; next comes the Llewyncyntefn reach of the Rev. Garnons Williams, covering a mile-and-a-quarter of the right bank ; there are ten pools, for some of which trousers are wanted. This fishing is sometimes let, but at the present period is in the owner's hands; then follows the Cwmwysk Genol Association water owned by Dr. Whittington, about a mile on the left bank with half-a-dozen pools, of which the best are the Quarry, the Middle, and the Park, all of them pretty certain to hold fish in autumn. From the top of this section right down to the tideway, trousers are always preferable to stockings. This is followed by the Park and Gelyno section, ownedby Miss Morgan, and then comes the Abercamlais water belonging to Mr. G. Williams, which covers about two miles, and is kept in the owner's hands. There are about nine good pools, the Turn, the Gutter, and the Shed, being the best; Miss Williams' Penpont section follows, about two miles of both sides down to Aberbraw Bridge, and then the right bank only; its seven good pools offer a nice day to one rod, and here Mr. John Hotchkis, the model Chairman of the Wye Board of Conservators, has a rod for two days in each week which go with his house of Pontarfran, at Brecon; the remaining days the owner keeps in her own hands. The Aberyseir fishing extends for half-a-mile on the left bank, and is usually let; the pool at the Yseir mouth is perhaps the best of the four or five in this section, which is owned by Mr. Rees Williams.

The Penwern Fishery of Mr. David Evans extends for nearly two miles, chiefly on both banks, and the owner keeps it in his own hands. Then just at Brecon comes the Newton Fishery, rented from Rev. G. Williams by the Association : it covers nearly three miles of both banks, and holds about ten good pools. Below Brecon is the Dinas Water, owned by Mr. J. Conway Lloyd, and partly rented by the Association and partly kept in owner's own hands ;

VOL. I. O '

altogether, there are about fourteen good pools, of which the best are perhaps those of the Turn, Coed Weir, the Boat, Cherry, and Glanusk. Sea trout ascend to all these upper waters, and, running from 2 to 8 Ibs., they take salmon flies and bait lures|of flies, the Doctor's, Jock Scotts, Butcher, Turkey wing with Peacock Herl body, and, indeed, almost any of the standard patterns, will kill for the first two or three days after a flood|then, as the river falls, worm, prawn and minnows are all used, though the first-named is the most deadly. Fish average about 10 Ibs. Below Dinas water comes Lord Glanusk's Peterston section, which is sometimes let. This is followed by Mr. T. P. Gwynne Holford's famous Buckland water. It is divided into three anglings : Buck- land, two-and-a-quarter miles on both sides, with three-quarters- of a mile on the right bank, is always kept in the hands of the owner. Scethrog and Gilestone are always let, and have never lacked a tenant. On the Buckland water there are eight good pools|the Railway Bridge, the Chain, Ashford Gravel and Wood, the Garden Stream and the Mill are all noted casts; on Scethrog and Gilestone, the Horse Shoe, Turn, Bend, and Boat are also well known. With favourable weather, June and July are the best months for salmon, while in March and April the trouting is usually of the very best. Here the Silver Grey, Jock Scott, Black Dose, with theCanary for high water and the Blue Doctor for low, are the favourite flies, and then worm, prawn, and minnow are also used. Sea trout are not plentiful, though a few appear towards the end of July. This section fishes best in rather low peat-stained water, and it keeps in order for a week after a flood. It was here that, some years ago, Mr. Alfred Crawshay caught 26 or 27 fish in a September day, while the keeper had 11 others.

At the foot of the Buckland water Mr. W. Partridge comes in for a short distance on the right bank, until Llan- gynider Bridge is reached, when the Duke of Beaufort comes in on the same side, and, keeping the water in his own hands, it is fished by those to whom he gives permission. On the opposite bank is the Gliffaes Angling of Lord Glanusk. Returning to the right bank, as the Duke's property ends Glanusk Park commences on both banks, and on the right one extends to Crickhowell Bridge, though on the left bank the Duke comes in again above the Bridge, and from this point His Grace's Llangattock Park water|let to Mr. Evans|runs on both banks, until it joins Colonel Robert Sandemann's Dan-y- Park Fishery, which extends for about two miles and nearly to the Chain Bridge at Llangrwyny. To my mind this is one of the best, if not the very best, on the river, though perhaps I may be prejudiced in its favourby reason of my good luck in having fished it as a guest of its happy owner, a " hard man " in sporting parlance only, ready at brief notice to ride steeplechases, hunt otters, catch salmon, trout, and poachers, or to use his rifle at a Bisley long range target or on Highland stags, quick and certain with his gun, and equally at home whether searching for a water-ouzel's nest in the river bank, or dangling over a cliff in mid-air to take a raven's nest, for some of these birds of unfrequented solitudes build within a few miles of Dan-y- Park. The trouting is quite on a par with the salmon fishing, and one day in a short half-hour I took a very level lot of thirteen beauties, scaling just as many pounds, from the Duke's Wood stream ; that was, however, nothing very extraordinary so far as my host was concerned, for every day he beat me pointless, and if I got 15 Ibs. of trout he always had three times that weight ; however, I am so constituted that if there is even but a remote chance of a salmon, then I *must* try for it to the neglect of the trout, however numerous they may be ; nevertheless, whenever I have said goodbye to my kind hostess at Dan-y- Park, I have always registered a mental vow that if, in some April to come, another opportunity was offered me, then I would refrain from taking out a salmon licence and devote myself entirely to making the best bag of trout that I could. On October

THE DUKE'S WOOD POOL, DAN-Y- PARK.

COLONEL R. P. SANDEMAN AT THE FARM POOL.

3rd, 1892, Colonel Sandeman killed with the fly and gaffed for himself, 22 fish weighing 236 Ibs., the heaviest 22 Ibs. ; they were rising well and hardly one was lost. On the day previous he had 8 fish averaging 11 Ibs., and on the 4th, another 6 of 12 Ibs. mean weight ; on the 5th,

13 others of 12 Ibs., and on the 6th he and his guests killed 1,009 rabbits in the Park, and on the 8th Colonel Sandeman rode at Kempton Park. Commencing again on

i/th October he had ... 7 salmon.

18th ... 5

igth ... 10

2ISt ... 5

22nd ,, ,, ... 9 ,,

3ist 10

ist November 13

On October loth, 1889, he took 18 fish which averaged

14 Ibs. 5 ozs., the heaviest 33 Ibs. ; all with the fly and all gaffed by himself; 16 of these fell to a fly of his own make, and it was only changed for a larger one as evening came on. The best afternoon he has had was in 1895, when commencing at 1.30 he took from the Farm andGlassllyn pools 17 salmon averaging just over n Ibs. ; ten days earlier he had had a day of 15 fish. The heaviest taken on this water was caught in May, 36 Ibs., and a real beauty! while as the angler was alone and had to carry it home for himself, there are those who declare he wished it lighter ere he reached the larder.

In the autumn of 1902 Colonel Sandeman was across the border seeking those "whose skins gleam red in the sunshine," and he only had five days at Dan-y- which yielded 43 fish, while his friends caught 20 others from October nth; from all this it will be seen that the Usk is not yet quite dead. In 1903 a nice lot of fish put in an appearance in May and June, but though water was wanted, the owner took more than 20 fish from one pool only, the heaviest of which was 31 Ibs. In his opinion the Usk is as good now as she ever was; the dominant droughts of the nineties beat the anglers, but with plenty of rain she would be as good as ever, though it would be still better if there were no netting on the Association waters at Usk, a barbarous method of adding to the funds of a rich Association, which must inevitably bring the best angling club in England into collision and disrepute with the whole of the river owners above the netting point. Below Dan-y- Park water proper on the left bank, the Duke of Beaufort, Colonel Parkinson, ColonelSandeman, and Sir E. Hamilton own short stretches; on the opposite right bank Miss Attwood, Colonel Parkinson, Mr. R. Crawshay, Mr. H. Gething, Mr. F. Humphrey also have fishing rights ; on the left bank, as Sir E. Hamilton's property ends the Marquess of Abergavenny joins in, and goes down to the town from which he takes his title, while

THE USK AT ABERGAVENNY.

the opposite bank belongs to Colonel Wheeley. The annexed rough sketch may, perhaps, serve best to show my readers how the anglings of this part of the Usk follow each other.

These reminiscences of the famous river are penned as the season of 1903 is drawing to a close; it has been a real good one, for rain has been plentiful, indeed too much so,

J. P. GWYNNE HOLFORD.

TALYBONT RAILWAY

Mr. Powell.

J. P. Gwynne Holford.

Mr. W. Partridge.

LI.ANGYNIDKR

Duke Of Beaufort.

Lord Glanusk.

The Park,

Crickhowki.i Duke Ok Beaufort.

Col. Sandeman,

Dan-y- Park,

Miss Attwood.

Col. Parkinson,

R. Crawshay

H. Gething.

F. Humphrvs.

Col. Wheelev

R Peterston. Lord Glanusk. *I V E R* J. P. Gwynne Holford. *u s A'* BRIDGE.±*Gliffaes, Let Abergavenny Toivn. forbythemiddleofSeptemberhundredsoffishhavepusheduppastB*

Chairman of the Board of Conservators: Mr. A. D. Berrington, Pant-y-Goitre, Abergavenny. Clerk : Colonel H. S. Lyne, Westgate Chambers, Newport.

The close time for nets is from ist September to ist March, and that for rods from 2nd November to ist March.

16

SECTION 16

Chapter XVI
SOUTH WALES

    The rivers falling into the north shores of the Bristol Channel and the Bays of Swansea and Carmarthen are, for the most part, worthless so far as salmon angling is concerned. They are the Ebbw, Rumney, Ely, Ogmore, Afon Llyfihi, Neath, with Dulas and Clydach, Tawe or Tave, Loughbr with Gwili, the two Gwendraeths, the Towy, Taf, the two Cleddaus, with several minor streams.

    On the right bank of its estuary, the Usk is joined by the Ebbw, from which pollutions have entirely wiped out the salmonidff that frequented it some sixty years ago in considerable numbers. Then crossing the Rumney and following the coast to the west we meet with the Taf and the Ely at Cardiff: all three of these streams are in a similar fishless state as the Ebbw, for in 1901 not one single salmon rod licence was issued for the Rumney or Ely and only one at 10s. 6d. for the Taf. Proceeding on our way we next come to the Ogmore with its tributaries, the AfonLlyffni and Ewenny, up which the old fishermen say that some sixty years ago there was every season a remarkable run of July and August sewin in which every fish was a female : in 1901 there were only six salmon rod licences issued for these three streams, which speaks more eloquently of their deterioration than a whole chapter of words could do. For a similar reason the Aber, Afon and the Neath, with its tributaries the Dulas and Clydach, must be left to join this list of rivers depleted of their fish by the pollutions from the vast and ever-increasing industries of this part of South Wales. The poison refuse of copper, lead, tin, iron and coal works has gained too much ground to. be interfered with now, and it is nearly certain that salmonida: will never again frequent any of these streams. Hurrying through Swansea for similar reasons we will pass by the Loughor and Gwili and the two Gwendraeths and make the best of our way to the Towy district, where the angler can once more put up his rod with confidence. In this area are the Loughor, the Gwendraeths, the Towy and the Taf; of these the Towy, with its tributaries Gwilli, Cothi, Sawdde, Gwdderig and Bran, is by far the most important. With a course of some sixty miles and a drainage area of 514 square miles, it flows from the wild and desolate bogs on the borders of Cardigan and Breconshire and for somedistance forms the march between these two counties : then entering Carmarthenshire near Capel Ystradffin and the cave of the freebooter Tom Jones, as it nears Llandovery it is joined by the Bran and Gwdderig; six miles lower down it flows by Llangadock and in about the same distance it reaches Llandilo and, passing through the estates of Lord Dynevor and the Earl of Cawdor's Golden Grove, in about a further fourteen miles it reaches Carmarthen, while during this part of its run it receives the contributions of the Cothi and Gwilli ; the former being the largest and most important of them all. After passing Carmarthen the Towy empties into a long trumpet-shaped estuary which eventually opens out into Carmarthen Bay.

In 1867 a Board of Conservators was formed and licences were issued for nets, coracles and all other fishing engines including rods, and forthwith the salmon, which were at this time at a very low ebb, began to increase.

In 1869 there were 70 rod licences issued in the whole district at 215. each, by far the larger number of them being for the Towy ; at this period the rod-fishers, for fear of having their angling rents raised, joined the ranks of the netters in declining to give any information as to their catches.

1870. There was a considerable increase in the take of fish to nets and rods ; 93 licences issued at 2is.

1871. 74 rod licences issued at 2 is.

1872. 97 rod licences issued at 21$.

1873. no rod licences at 215. In this year the proprietors on the Cothi subscribed together to purchase and pull clown the weir at Cothi Bridge, which had hitherto unduly obstructed the free passage of fish to the upper waters ; and as this river is some thirty miles in length with excellent pools and spawning grounds, the owners were speedily rewarded for their enterprise.

1874. 97 rod licences at 2is., who between them captured about 200 salmon and sea trout. The latter averaged about a pound each, and the heaviest salmon scaled 24- lbs.

1875. 88 rod licences at 21.; this was a very dry season ; the rod catch was small and not ascertainable. The Board of Conservators estimated that there were fully 180 men netting the river for seven months every year, and that at a moderate estimate each would earn $20 in that time ; this gives a total sum of .$3,600, and so, if sea trout *and salmon were lumped together and taken 6s. 6d. a fish, the total catch of the nets would work out at about 10,000 fish per season, perhaps 4,000 salmon and grilse and 6,000 sewin.*

1876. 117 rod licences at 21$.; this was a good rod season ; on the Edwinsford section of the Cothi, where one angler had 15 salmon in two September days, another Vol. r.

had 18 in a few days ; and a third in October had nine in two days. Mr. Benyon of Trewern killed up to the 17th September, 17 salmon, largest 18 Ibs., and 44 sewin, fifteen of the latter scaling over 3 Ibs.; this bag was made on the Taf or Tave. There was, however, a general consensus of opinion that angling ought to end on ist October, instead of on the 3151 of the month, for even as early as the 2Oth of September, many of the fish that were landed were returned by good sportsmen as quite unfit to be eaten.

1877. 135 rod licences at 2is. ; this was a poor season, and no one rod had more than ten fish. There was some friction with the coracle men on the subject of raising their licence duty ; these coracle nets date back from the very- earliest days, and Wales is their birthplace ; the net is worked between two coracles (much on the same principle as the trap nets of the Suir and other Irish rivers) ; a man in each coracle floats down stream with the net suspended between them, and as soon as an ascending salmon strikes it, it is instantly pulled into a bag by means of rings working on strings, somewhat after the manner in which window curtains are pulled together. At this period there were some sixty of these coracles working in the district, but chiefly in the Towy. They were regarded as objectionable nets, as they wereworked in fresh water and could only capture fish which, having escaped the perils of the sea nets, the anglers and river owners maintained should be free from further persecution so far as nets were concerned

1879. 142 rod licences at 2is. ; 1,745 trout rod licences at is. The salmon rods took from 150 to 200 salmon, and about 1,250 sewin, with a few bull trout. From the middle of January to the middle of February, there is every season a small run of " Glasbach " as the natives call them, fish of about 8 Ibs., which correspond with the "Blue Cocks" of the Wye and Usk.

1880. 163 rod licences at 2is.; they took about 50 salmon and 200 sewin.

1881. 150 rod licences at 215. ; they caught about 300 salmon averaging 7 Ibs., and 750 sewin averaging 2- Ibs. ; there was an unusually heavy run of grilse. The upper owners of the Towy complained that since the destruction of the Cothi Bridge Weir they got much less fish, as now that the Cothi Weir ceased to obstruct the river, the fish appeared to prefer the Cothi to the Towy.

1882. 174 rod licences at 2 is. ; the nets took about 74,000 Ibs. of fish ; the rods caught about 400 salmon average 10 Ibs., and 1,800 sea trout weighing 2,700 Ibs. On the Cothi and Taf, sport was especially good.

1883. 208 rod licences at 2 is. ; 1,579 trout licences at 2s. 6d. The nets took 112,000 Ibs. of fish. The rods caught about 500 salmon of lolbs. and 2,500 sewin weighing 3,750 Ibs. This was the best season since the formation of the Board of Conservators. There was a slight outbreak of disease, and also vigorous attacks were made on the pike, which had been allowed to become much too plentiful. At this period the close time for nets was from the ist September to 1 5th March; for rods, from 2nd November to i5th March. Mr. P. Benyon, of Trewern, was the Chairman of the Board.

1884. 173 rod licences at 2 is. The nets took 115,000 Ibs. of salmonida ; rods caught about 200 salmon of 10 Ibs. and 500 sewin of i\- Ibs. Though this was a very dry season 15 rods at Llandilo caught 121 salmon and 91 sewin.

1885. 159 rods at 2is. ; their catch not ascertainable. The nets took 76,160 Ibs. from the tidal part of the Towy, and this does not include the catch of the coracle men. About 50 pike were destroyed by the Water-bailiffs.

1886. 148 licences at 21.; 1,541 trout licences at 2s. 6af.

1887. 124 licences at 2 is. A very dry season, and returns of nets and rods not reported.

1888. 158 licences at 215. The weekly close time was extended from forty-two to forty-eight hours.

1889. 134 licences at 215.

1890. 107 licences at 2 is. ; 1,615 trout licences at 2s. 6d. The nets took 12,200 Ibs. of fish.

1891. 125 licences at 2 is. ; 1,897 trout licences at 2s. 6d. The nets took 19,000 Ibs. of salmon and 18,762 Ibs. of sewin. No returns of rod catch, though said to be much above the average. Some disease appeared.

1892. 117 licences at 215. Season for nets and rods about the average. The nets took 24,907 Ibs. of salmon and 33,277 Ibs. of sewin. A proposal of the netters to lengthen the netting season was vetoed.

1893. 99 licences at 2 is. A very bad season all round.

$ s. d.

1894. 105 rod licences at 2is. = 110 5 o

1,848 trout licences at 2.y. 6d. = 231 o o

34i 5 o

Licence duty for nets and coracles 159 8 6 These are remarkable figures, as they show that the Towy anglers contribute considerably more than twice as much money for the preservation of the river than do the netters, and yet the latter get at least 20 fish for the one of the angler. Thus, if there were no anglers, and the netting licences formed the only preservation fund, it is nearly certain that the catch of the netters would be reduced to next to nothing. This is something that is not sufficiently brought

VOL. I.

to the notice of the netters, who as a body regard every suggestion made by the anglers for the betterment of a river as directly hostile to their interests : it would seem from these figures that, without the anglers, the netters of the Towy would soon be in a sorry plight.

1895. 74 licences at 21.; 1,726 trout at 2s. 6d.; nets took about 46,794 Ibs. of fish. No returns of rods.

1896. 72 rod licences at 215.; a very dry season and angling poor.

1897. 8 licences at 2is. ; 2,042 trout licences at 25. 6d.

1898. 89 licences at 215.

1899. 63 licences at 2is. ; a very dry season and, so, poor angling.

1900. 89 licences at 2is. ; again a very dry season; the netting season altered and close time to commence on ist September and continue to ist April. Rods to cease 15th October until ist April.

1901. 76 licences at 2is. ; 1,930 trout licences at 2s. 6d.; No returns from nets or rods.

1902. 89 licences at 2is. ; 2,331 trout ditto at 2s. 6d. ; No returns.

From these returns it will be seen that in the ten years from 1890 to 1899 the salmon rod licences have averaged 87 per season, while in the previous ten years they averaged158 per season; this serious falling off clearly indicates that there is something wrong somewhere in the administration of the Fishery which requires the immediate attention of the Government Inspector and the Board of Conservators. The chief riparian owners of the Towy are Mr. Schaw-Protheroe, Trewern, Whitland ; Judge T. Bishop, Dollgarreg, Llandovery; The Earl Cawdor, Golden Grove, Llandilo; Mr. A. Campbell Davys, Neuaddfawr, Llandovery; The Lord Dynevor, Dynevor Castle, Llandilo; Mr. Evans, Dayle House, Llandilo; Mr. C. W. Mansel Lewis, Stradey Castle, Llanelly ; Mr. Mervyn Peel, Danyralt, Llangadock; Miss Thursby Pelham, Aber- marlais Park, Llangadock ; Mr. J. C. Richardson, Glanbrydon Park, Manordeilo; and J. Lewis Thomas, Caeglas, Llandilo. From Llandovery to Llandilo there is a good bit of free angling, and even where it is preserved the owners, if absent, will often, as at Danyralt and Llanwrda, kindly give leave for a day. Below Llandilo Earl Cawdor keeps the water in his own hands, though lower down tickets for a part of it can be had from the " Golden Grove Arms" at Llanarthney\icw. for the season, is. per day. Also there is an Angling Association at Carmarthen, Mr. F. Trevitt, Francis Terrace, being the Secretary, and another at Llandilo, but inasmuch as I wrote to each of them asking for the Rules, etc., of their respective clubs, and received no reply fromeither, it may, perhaps, be assumed that these clubs have been dissolved.

The Cothi is all in the hands of the riparian owners. Mr. M. L. VV. Lloyd-Price owns about 2 miles of the right bank at Bryn Cothi-Nantgaredig, and then both sides for about 250 yards; in his absence it is at times let and holds eight salmon pools, which are fished chiefly from the bank, though stockings are useful for some of them and for crossing the river; it will carry two rods easily and all over the river a rod of 16 ft. is ample. The Cliff, The Rhyd and the NantyfHn Pools are the three best. July is the best sewin time and later for salmon. The Doctors, Jock Scott and silver bodies do best, quite small size, but all lures are permitted, and in suitable water the worm is very killing ; fish average about 9 Ibs. and as many as a dozen have been caught in ten days, while 27 sea trout in a day by Mr. Fry is the record of recent years. Large brown trout flies such as March Brown, Blue, and the Yellow Dun are as good as any. The Cothi keeps in order for three or four days after a flood ; there is also very good April trouting on the river here and in the brooks of the estate ; two rods had in twenty-two days of April, 1903, just over 800 trout. Other proprietors are General Sir J. Hills Johnes, G.C.B., at Dolancothi; Sir James Drummond, Bt., at Edwinsford ; andColonel Gwynne Hughes at Glancothi. Of the other streams of the district the Taf, which falls into the Towy estuary, often yields good sport, and is closely preserved. Then close to Kidwilly the Gwendraeth Fach and Gwendraeth Fawr, with a watershed of seventy-three square miles, empty themselves into the sea. The Fawr or "Big" river is the more southern of the two ; it has a run of but eleven miles, while oddly enough the Fach or " Little " river has a course of fifteen miles, and thus the two streams present one of those strange cases where the "Big" is less than the "Little." The Fawr is not preserved; the Fach is more of a sewin than a salmon stream, and both rivers suffer from the pollution of tin plate works. The Loughor, flowing into the Burry Inlet of Carmarthen Bay, is sixteen miles in length with a drainage area of 156 squard miles; it suffers greatly from the pollutions of coal, copper and iron, which are so bad that the river is only preserved in a few places. Fifty or sixty years ago this river was famous for its very large sea trout, many of them scaling from 10 to 14 Ibs.; then in the early sixties the river was desperately poached all the year round, and though attempts were made to form Angling Clubs, every effort in that direction was doomed to fail, and there is but small doubt that the Loughor will ultimately join the ranks of the Ebbw, Rom- ney, Neath and the other fishless streams of South Wales.

The East and West Cleddau or Cleddy between them drain an area of 326 square miles. The Western river rises near St. Catherines, and after a course of twenty-four miles falls into the long, narrow and winding estuary of Milford Haven, a few miles below Haverfordwest. The Eastern river, flowing from the Precelli Hills, with a run of twenty miles, falls into another arm of the Y shaped estuary at Conaston Bridge, and up to about 1860 the salmonidff of the two streams were netted by some sixty to seventy boats working in the tidal water; very small-meshed nets were used, the close season was wholly disregarded, while each river had a "slaughter box," as the natives aptly named it, in a cruive fixed in a mill dam; then above these dams the many coracle nets swept up the few fish that had contrived to escape the dangers below ; poaching was rampa'nt and every farm-hand had his spear, and rarely did a spawning fish ever return to the sea; to add to the destruction the shed or smolts were taken by basketsful and openly sold. In 1866 a Board of Conservators was formed, who in 1876 issued five salmon rod licences at los. 6d., and in the last week of November two fish were actually caught by rod weighing 14 Ibs. and 8 Ibs., while two coracle nets working above the dam took thirty pounds' worth of salmon and sewin. The main harvest in both rivers was always inSeptember and October, though occasional clean fish were caught as early as April.

1869. 13 rod licences at los. 6d. The "stop" or " compass" nets were declared illegal. These nets were worked by fixing a boat across the stream in much the same way as the Thames fisherman fixes his punt, a bag net is then let out under the boat, the mouth being kept open partly by long poles and partly by the rush of the tides; as soon as a fish enters the net and strikes the bag end, the mouth is instantly raised above water by strings worked by the two men in the boat.

1870. 30 rod licences at los. 6d.; about 100 salmon were caught in the West river.

1871. 31 rod licences at los. 6d.; about 70 salmon caught in each river.

1872. ii rod licences at los. dd.; no returns.

1873. 22 Iqs. 6d.

1874. 25 Iqs. 6d.

1875. J4 ,, iCtf- 6d.

1876. 15 Iqs. 6d.

1877. 10 ios. 6d.

1878. 18 ios. 6d.

At this date the close time for nets was from i5th September to i5th March, for rods from 2ist November to15th March. Colonel Owen of Haverfordwest was Chairman of the Board.

1879. 18 rod licences at 105. 6d.; 225 trout licences at 35-. 6d.

1880. 24 rod licences at los. 6d.

1881. 28 ,, ios. 6d.

1882. 31 ,, los. 6d.

1883. 39 ,, ios.' 6d. The two rivers yielded 80 salmon to the rods.

1884. 38 rod licences at 10.?. 6d. A very good season and more salmon seen than for many years. The rods .of the two rivers took about 250 fish.

1885. 34 licences at ios. 6d. ; 224 trout licences at 35. 6d. The rods captured 208 fish.

1886. 24 licences at ios. 6d. The rods caught 226 fish.

1887. In this year the "Great Net," which had been abolished from the mouth of the Teifi as illegal, was brought to Milford Haven Estuary and worked there. On the 26th and 27th of August it captured 280 fish in two hauls and more than 2,000 before the end of the season.

1888. 24 rod licences at ios. 6d. ; they caught close on loo salmon.

1889. 24 licencees took about 120 fish.

1890. 27 licences at los. 6d. ; 247 trout licences at 3$. 6d. 126 salmon taken in the two streams.

1891. 26 licences at ioy. 6d.

1892. 18

1893. 21 5. they took 148 fish.

1894- 19

1895. 12 .. ii they took 160 fish.

1896. 13

1897. 12

1898. 6

1899. 8

1900. 4 ,, ,, a very bad season.

1901. 7 licences at icw. del., 201 trout licences at $s. 6el., 14 fortnight at 2s. 6d., 8 weekly at is.

From these statistics it is easy to gather that the salmon angling of the two Cleddaus has rapidly deteriorated; in the four years from 1882 to '85 the Conservators issued a total of 142 rod licences at Iqs. 6d. each; then for the four years 1894 to 1897 the total fell to 56 licences, while for the following four years of 1898 to 1901 they declined to the insignificant total of 25! Therefore, if in a rich and populous district through which flow two very pretty salmon streams each of which formerly abounded in fish, there cannot be found more than half-a-dozen anglers who are willing to payios. 6d. each for their rod licence, then indeed may the streams of that district be described in the terse language of the schoolboy as having "gone to pot".

My readers may perhaps feel surprised that these streams should be described as once having " abounded" with salmon, but I think the term is warranted having regard to the fact that in 1884 they yielded 250 fish to the rods from a drainage area of 326 square miles, while in the same year the Usk, the best salmon river in England, with a drainage area of 634 square miles only yielded 825 fish to the rods.

Close time for nets from i5th September to i5th March; for rods from ist November to ist February.

Chairman of Board of Conservators: Mr. J. C. Yorke, Langton, Durbach, Pembroke. Clerk: Mr. R. T. P. Williams, High Street, Haverfordwest.

17

SECTION 17

Chapter XVII
THE TEIFI

Rises from the hill of Briddell on the borders of Radnorshire, and taking a south-westerly course it flows past Tregaron, from whence passing on to Lampeter to be joined by the Dulais, it becomes a comparatively big river; then with a further run of twenty miles it arrives at Newcastle Emlyn, fifteen miles above Cardigan, where the Teifi, after a total run of some seventy miles, with a catchment basin of 389 square miles, expands into a long pottle-shaped estuary, which eventually opens out into Cardigan Bay. In 1862, this estuary was hard fished by sixteen draught nets, while a fixed net was used in the river itself down to the bridge at Cardigan, and again, above this, other nets were worked, locally known as "jackass nets." Then the river between Llechrhyd (five miles above Cardigan) and Cenarth Bridge, a length of about six miles, was closely fished by 300 coracles, the men basing their claims to do this by right of long and undisputed usage ; then at the very top of all these obstacles there was a salmon trap at Cenarth Weir ; thus it was only above this last obstruction that the riparian owners began to exercise their rights, while at this period it was stated on good authority that in proportion to its size, more nets were used on the Teifi than

---

on any other river in England or Wales. The actual fixed obstructions were very few, the two principal ones being the Mill Weir above Cenarth Bridge, with another one at Newcastle Emlyn. In 1860, the close time for nets did not commence till the 3rd of November, and was only partially observed; spears and lights were ceaselessly plied on the spawning beds, while fry was openly captured and openly sold throughout the district; in addition to these drawbacks, the river was seriously threatened by the pollutions from four lead mines that had commenced work near its source. In 1861 an Angling Association was formed to protect the fish and generally improve the angling, but this was compelled to break up in the year following for lack of funds.

THE TEIFI AT NEWCASTLE EMLYN.

1867. A Board of Conservators was formed.

A CORACLE RACE.

1868. A very dry season, and scarcely a salmon was captured by rod. The Conservators commenced to blow up the obstructive rocks at Cenarth, but the natives stoned the workmen off the river, and as soon as they had been routed, their tools, barrows, and planks, were broken to pieces and thrown into the water. 23 salmon rod licences issued at 2os. each; 23 seine nets at 3is. 6d. ; 91 coracles at ids. 6d.

VOL. I.

The fishermen, who had hitherto netted without any payment for their licences, resented the tax, and vowed that they would fish the whole Teifi next year without any licences at all.

1869. By the opening of the season a better feeling prevailed amongst the netters, who had begun to recognize that stricter preservation would quickly mean more profit. The refuse from the Cilgerran slate quarries had by degrees so filled up the bed of the river that, at low water, salmon had to thread their way through masses of slate ; also the obstruction at the Cenarth Fall remained as bad as ever, the river being greatly damaged thereby. The quantity and the quality of Teifi salmon was proverbial throughout Wales : Teifi salmon. Usk trout, and Lugg eels were ever mentioned as the three greatest fish delicacies the Principality could offer. Very heavy floods in summer enabled the rods to gel a few fish. 31 salmon rod licences at 20.?.

1870. 32 salmon rod licences at 2os.; a very dry season, but the rods took from 80 to 100 salmon, but in this is included the take from the Ayron river, which at this date was embraced in the Teifi district.

1871. 42 rod licences at 2cw. ; no reports,

1872. 37 i

44)

1874. 37 rod licences at -2os. ; no reports. The netters at length began to realize that the Act of 1861 was passed in their best interests and not in opposition to them.

1875. 44 rod licences at 205. Heavy floods took a good stock of fish to the upper waters.

1876. 44 rod licences at 20.

1877. 52 rod licences at 2cw. More than 200 salmon caught by rod at Teifi and Ayron. At the end of this season the Ayron and Arth were formed into a separate district.

1878. 44 rod licences at 20s.

1879. The close time at this period was, for nets, from ist September to ist February; for rods, from 15th October to ist February ; while no gaff might be carried prior to ist April. There were great complaints of mine pollution. It was decided to raise the rod licence duty from 20. to

1880. 68 rod licences at 30s. They caught about 300 fish.

1 88 1. 39 rod licences at 30s. They only got about 20 fish : the nets took 87,360 Ibs. of salmon. The rod licence was again altered, and reduced to 20$. : monthly and fortnightly licences were also issued.

1882. 72 rod licences at 20. ; 3 rod licences, month, at los. fd. 24 rod licences, fortnight, at 55. ; 722 rod licencesat 25. 6d. A slight amount of disease appeared. Close time for rods altered from 15th October to ist February to 15th November to i4th February, and the gaff was permitted to be carried throughout the open season.

1883. 56 rod licences at 2os.; i rod licence, month, at Iqs. 6d. ; 24 rod licences, fortnight, at 55. This was a good angling year, but no returns were made. Most of the north Cardigan lead mines had ceased to work, and many people attributed the increased supply of salmon to the cessation of their pollution.

1884. 57 licences at zos.; 2 licences at los. ; 25 licences at 5.

1885. 64 licences at 20s.; i licence at los.; 39 licences at $s.

1886. 53 licences at 2os. ; 5 licences at Iqs. 6d. ; 53 licences at 55. The rod close time was again changed, and from this date it was to be from 2Oth October to ist February.

1887. 44 licences at 2os. ; 3 licences at los. 6d. ; 33 licences at 55. At this date there were 23 draught nets at work in the estuary and 40 coracle nets working above Cardigan up to Coedmore, where the tideway now ended, though formerly it used to go as far as Llechrydd

1888. No returns of the number of licences issued. The rods took from 90 to 100 salmon.

1889. 63 licences at 20s. ; 6 licences at los. 6al. ; 42 licences at $s. ; 304 trout licences at u. The trout licence was reduced from 2s. 6d. to is.

1890. 57 licences at 20s. ; 5 licences at los. 6d. ; 45 licences at 55.

1891. 60 licences at 2os. ; 5 licences at icw. 6d. ; 44 licences at 55.

1892. 52 licences at 20. ; 2 licences at os. 6d. ; 42 licences at 55. A very dry season.

1893. 42 licences at 2os. ; i licence at los. 6d. ; 19 licences at $s. A dry and bad season, with considerable disease.

1894. 48 licences at 20. ; i licence at los. 6d. ; 30 licences at 5.

1895. 41 licences at 2os. ; i licence at icw. 6d.; 24

licences at 5. In this year the riparian owners, the anglers and the coracle fishermen proposed that a bye-law should be made for the abolishment of the " shot fawr," or great net, that was worked at the mouth of the Teifi. It had for long been the custom of the draught-net fishermen in the public waters below Cardigan to take it in turn to join two of their nets together, and to use the long net thus formed in a different way to the ordinary manner in which the other

VOL. I. Q

draught nets were worked. In this mode of fishing each of the twenty draught nets in the estuary would get its chance of becoming the "Shot Fawr" once in every five days. The two nets when joined made a length of nearly four hundred yards, which was stretched and fixed across the top of the estuary, and so every salmon that fell back with the tide was caught by it, and as many as 170 had been taken at one shot. In times of continued drought this net was, therefore, certain to capture the whole of the fish that had gathered together when waiting for a flood. Therefore complaints were made to the Fishery Inspector that the great killing power of this net was ruining the fisheries of the Teifi ; the coracle fishers were especially loud in their denunciations and pointed out how largely their numbers had diminished, while the anglers, following suit, declared it useless to take out rod licences, and they brought evidence to prove that less than twenty years ago it was not uncommon for a rod to take four or five fish in a day, whereas in recent years it was rare for an individual angler to catch five fish in the whole season. The hotel-keepers of the neighbourhood also joined in the outcry, as they complained bitterly of the loss of custom following on the great decrease in the number of the angling visitors, and they handed in a list of the names of forty-two rod licence holders in the Llandyssil neighbourhood which showed that out of thirty-nine of them only one had caught two fish in the season of 1894, that two anglers had caught one fish each, and that the remaining thirty-six had caught nothing. The petitioners also pointed out that though the river was greatly over netted that was not the sole cause of the deterioration. The poaching of spawning salmon in the upper waters, and of the fry in their

NETTING AT TEIFI MOUTH.

descent to the sea, which were openly sold in the streets of Cardigan at fourpence a pound, also contributed largely to the decay ; then, in their turn, the supporters of the " Shot Fawr" reproached the upper proprietors for the laxness of their preservation of the upper waters ; a reproach which was met with the retort that so long as the lower nets caught nearly all the fish, there was no inducement to preserve the very few that survived to spawn. After much discussion the " Shot Fawr" was eventually doomed and ceased to exist in the following year.

1896. 41 licences at 205.; 3 licences at Ids. 6d. ; 40 licences at $s. A poor season.

1897. 46 licences at 205. ; 13 licences at los. 6d. These licence duties, together with those of the nets, did not produce funds sufficient for the thorough protection of the river. The rod close time was again altered and from this season was fixed to begin on ist November and end on the ist February.

1898. 52 licences at 20. ; 20 at Iqs. The fortnightly- ones were done away with. As there were only four bailiffs for the protection of 386 square miles, meetings were held at Cardigan and at Llandyssil to consider what steps could be taken to improve the fishery. This was a year of water- plenty and more fish were seen between Llandyssil and Lampeter than for many years; the draught nets had a fish of 30 Ibs., the cofcacle men one of 27 Ibs. and an angler one of 26 Ibs. : ten tons of salmon were sent away by the Great Western Railway, to which must be added the local sales.

1899. 43 rod licences at zos. ; n at los. 6d. The nets sent away 27,330 Ibs., the rods caught 23 salmon ranging from 10 to 15 Ibs.

1900. A great improvement and a good season. Complaints were made that the fines inflicted on poachers were too trifling to act as deterrents ; especially the fines imposed for second and third offences. The nets took 31,420 Ibs. of salmon, the rods caught 70 fish weighing 770 Ibs. 38 licences at 20$. ; 27 at 10s. 6d. ; 1,024 trout licences at 2s. 6d.

1901. 51 licences at 2os. ; 37 at 10s. 6d. The nets took 1,500 fish averaging close on 18 Ibs., the rods caught 82 salmon averaging 12 Ibs. the two heaviest 21 and 20 Ibs.

1902. 50 licences at 2O.y. ; 55 month at 10s. 6d. The nets took 21,072 Ibs. of salmon. The rods took 168 salmon weighing 2,184 Ibs. ; largest to net 33 Ibs., to rod 26 Ibs. ; largest sea trout 7 Ibs.

In 1894 there were 23 draught nets and 27 coracle nets at work : in this season there were only 11 draught nets and 17 coracle nets.

The salmon fishings of the Teifi lie between the top of the tideway and Lampeter, a distance of about thirty miles, and in favourable seasons the cream of it is between Llandyssil and Lampeter ; the chief proprietors are the Earl of Cawdor and Mr. Charles Fitzwilliams at Newcastle Emlyn, Colonel Lewes of Llysnewydd, Colonel Davies Evans of Highmead, Llanybyther, Mr. G. M. Hodding of Llanfair House, Llandyssil, and Mr. J. C. Harford of Falcondale, Lampeter; this last mentioned fishery is seven-and-a-half miles in length, of which two-and-a-half are on one side only and lie immediately above Lampeter Bridge, then following on and below the bridge there is a further two-and-a-half miles of both banks; above the bridge there are five good pools, while below it are fourteen others of which the Soldier, Brickyard, Billy Morris and Jenken's Back are very good, though there are others quite as tempting, but with Welsh names that in spelling and pronunciation are most puzzling to the poor Sassenach. A rod of 16 ft. will cover all the water, for which no waders are required; very few grilse are got, while only three sea trout have been recorded in the past twenty years. The gaff may be carried throughout the season, and though all lures are permitted it is seldom that salmon are caught by any other one than the fly, the favourites being Durham-Ranger, Jock, Blue Doctor, the Teifi, the Colonel and St. Davids. The Falcondale water yields from 15 to 50 fish averaging 12 Ibs. ; of these only a few, unless there are copious summer rainfalls, are got before the nets come off on ist September. A dry month all along the Teifi means poor sport. Mr. Har.ford keeps his angling in his own hands, but generously gives permission to visitors staying at the " Black Lion " Hotel at Lampeter. At Llanfair House, Llandyssil, Mr. G. M. Hodding has the exclusive right of four miles on one bank (the other being strictly preserved) in which there are twenty good casts ; in periods of water-plenty there are fish up here by the end of April, though the bulk of the sport is had in September and October, which in favourable seasons should yield from 20 to 40 fish. As Mr. Hodding sometimes lets Llanfair House, so prettily placed, so comfortable and so well furnished, it may interest my readers to know that the trouting is also good, especially in the spring ; while, helped by the shooting of a large rookery in May, otter hounds in June, rabbits galore in July and August, with a considerable extent of mixed shooting from September ist, the non-fishing days may be most happily spent. The proprietor of the " Forth " Hotel at Llandyssil, Mr. A. E. Smith, owns about five-and-a- half miles of the Teifi, which is at the disposal of his visitors ; there are four miles above the hotel on the right bank which holds seventeen good pools, and then there is another mile below the hotel in which there are four or five casts; the opposite banks are preserved and fished by their owner. Waders are hardly wanted and very few anglers wear them.All lures are allowed ; the favourites, if the fly proves useless, being the Devon minnow and the worm. There are a very few sewin caught in July, while there are plenty of "Brownies." In 1902 the total take of salmon was 40; in 1903 four spring fish had been taken up to the 28th April. The Llysnewydd Water belonging to Colonel Lewes is about half-way between Llandyssil and Newcastle Emlyn, and here the Teifi broadens and deepens into a bigger river; this section runs for about two miles on the right bank and for between three and four on the left, and is always kept in the hands of the owner. Some of the pools can be cast from the bank, and in big water trousers command the others more easily than stockings, while a rod of 18 ft. can be used; perhaps the best pools are those of the Henfryn, Coedstrae, Penraltfachnog, Llynbadell and Pwllglas. The fly is the only lure permitted, with May the best month for spring fish ; bull trout up to 6 Ibs. have several times been caught by Mr. W. Lewes on the Henllan section of this fishery, and also in some seasons a few sea trout.

This is such a remarkable average weight that it is probably a printer's error which has escaped the usually vigilant eyes of the censor of the Fishery Board Reports. I think it is intended to be 8 Ibs. not 18 Ibs.

The " Salutation" Hotel at Newcastle E-mlyn offers its visitors free angling on the Earl of Cawdor's section, which includes both banks, holding four or five good pools, none of them very far from the Hotel; all lures are allowed, wadersnot necessary. Part of the opposite bank is preserved and owned by Mr. C. H. L. Fitzwilliams of Cilgwyn ; this fishing extends from the Bridge for two miles on the north bank, (with the exception of the " Emlyn Arms" meadow, rented from the Earl Cawdor); there are six good pools in this section, mostly fishable from the bank, viz. : Blaenant Run, Danwarren, the Lamb, and the Rocks below the weir; in the spring, salmon do not rest for long in these pools, where September and October are the best months. Silver Doctor, Jock Scott, the Invincible (a black and gold-bodied fly), and then flies with claret bodies such as the Gordon, are also favourites with Mr. Fitzwilliams ; medium size from No. i Limerick downwards. There are very few sea trout and what there are are generally caught after July; salmon average 12 Ibs., and grilse 4 to 5 Ibs. Higher up the Teifi at Llandyssil, Mr. Fitzwilliams is also the owner of about half-a-mile of both banks; a nice piece of water extending from the mouth of the Turley burn on the south side down to the meadow below the church on the north side, in which is the Church Meadow Pool ; then there are three other good casts on this water, which is let to the " Cilgwyn Arms " Hotel, close to the railway station.

Over-netting and poaching are the drawbacks to Teifi angling, and if these evils were mitigated then the Teifi wouldbe one of the best of salmon rivers. Even as it is, some good autumn takes have been made, for when angling above Llandyssil, Mr. Lascelles, Colonel Lewes, and Mr. Fitz- williams, have each killed six fish in the day; improved drainage causes the rains to run off more quickly than they formerly did, and in dry summers very few fish manage to pass the draught nets plying at the mouth, or the coracle men working in the fresh water that lies between Cenarth Weir and the tideway. Perhaps a prolongation of the weekly close time by a further twelve hours would stimulate owners, hotel- keepers, and anglers, to provide a stronger force of watchers during the spawning season ; at any rate an addition of twelve hours to the weekly stop would be certain to help the river without inflicting any great hardship on the netters or coracle men.

The Chairman of the Board is Mr. E. Robinson, Boncath, Pembrokeshire; Clerk: Mr. H. W. Howell, Bank House, Lampeter.

Close time for rods, from November ist to February 28th; for nets, from September ist to February ist.

18

SECTION 18

Chapter XVIII
THE AYRON AND ARTH

The first-named stream falls into Cardigan Bay at Aberayron, some twenty miles to the north of the Teifi ; up to 1860 the tidal water was publicly fished by about fifteen pole nets using a very small mesh, but as the 1861 Act rendered them illegal they disappeared in 1862. The Ayron has a narrow shallow channel, and at the top of the tideway there was in those days a fishing mill dam in which there was no pass, while on the shore to the north of the river mouth there were many semi-circular stone weirs, locally known as " Goryds" and anglicised into " Gogheads"; they are much the same sort of weirs as are placed in other rivers, which are variously known as gurths, baulks and hangs. The Ayron is naturally a .good salmon stream, although it has but a course of fifteen miles, and drains but fifty-two square miles. The Arth is a small stream falling into the sea a few miles to the north of the Ayron, and is more used by sea trout than by salmon. Up to 1882 both rivers were included in the Teifi district, but in 1881 the riparian owners of the Ayron andArth petitioned that the two streams might be formed into a separate district. They also asked for some alterations in the close time and that the issue of trout licences should be discontinued, and, to show

how much they were in earnest, they declared that, if their petition was not granted, they would withdraw assistance in every form to the Board of Conservators. Thus in 1883 the two streams under discussion were formed into a separate district, which I think is the smallest one in England or Wales. In this year the new Board issued 18 salmon rod licences at 2os., 2 monthly at Iqs. and 13 weekly licences at 5. There was considerable poaching, which the Board were not able to cope with for want of funds.

1884. 19 licences at 20. ; 2 at los. ; 16 at 55.

1885. n ,, 2os. ; 3 at los.; 9 at 55.

1886. The weirs at Aberayron and Llyswrn were carried away by winter floods, and fish passes were ordered to be made in the fresh ones.

1887. 7 licences at 20.9. ; 2 at los. ; 6 at 5.

1888. 13 licences at 205. ; i at los.; 13 at 5$. 144 trout licences produced $16. 35. od.

1889. 13 licences at zos. ; 2 at los. ; 16 at 5.

1890. 4 licences at 2os. ; 3 at los. ; 12 at 5. When the weirs were rebuilt it was found that the work had beenimproperly done, and the Fishery Board threatened to prosecute.

1891. 4 licences at 20. ; 9 at los. ; 31 at 5.

1892. The use of draught nets was forbidden in the narrow channel between the two piers at Aberayron.

1893. 4 licences at 20. ; 3 at icxr. ; 17 at 5$. ; 95 trout licences at 2s. 6d. ; very dry season.

1894. The season rod licence was reduced from 205. to i os.. and fortnightly ones were issued at 5$. 23 of the former and 9 of the latter were issued. The trout licence, of which 256 were issued, was reduced from 2s. 6d. to is.

1895. 16 licences at los. ; 12 at 5.; autumn sport good; less poaching than in previous years.

1896. 15 licences at 105-.; 7 at 5$.

1897. 10 10

1898. 8 12

1899. 16 licences at Ids. ; 6 at 5$. ; 261 trout licences at is.

1900. 15 at Iqs. ; 13 at 5$.

1901. 16 at los. ; 16 at 5$.

1902. 22 at los. ; 9 fortnight at 55.

It will be seen that the reduction in the cost of the rod licences was a total failure and resulted in a considerable loss to the funds of the Conservators.

VOL. I.

It is remarkable that the head Water-bailiff of this District, after having made eighteen annual returns to his Board, has entirely ignored the question put to him every year : " Can you give an estimate of the number and weight of salmon and sea trout caught with net and by rod" ? The returns of the nets have ever been difficult to procure, but it is indeed extraordinary that the bailiff on a stream, if only fifteen miles in length, should not have been able to say something more or less definite as to the rod catch. Wading stockings are useful, and the flies that are used on the Teifi will kill here.

The close time for nets is from ist September to ist February ; for rods from i5th November to I4th February.

The Chairman of the Board is Major Price Lewes, Ty Glyn Aeron, Ciliau-Aeron, R.S.O., Cardiganshire.   Clerk to the Board: Mr. E. Lima Jones, Bridge Street, Aberayron.

Chapter XIX

THE DOVEY, MAWDDACH, ARTRO, DWYRYD, PRYSOR, AND GLASLYN

To the north of the Arth the streams of Ystwith and Rheidol fall into Cardigan Bay at Aberystwith, and though formerly each held salmon and sewin in some numbers, the pollutions from various mines have quite wiped them out, and now-a- days these pretty streams may be compared to two sewers, used almost solely for the lawless and selfish benefit of industries which could well afford to take proper means to effectually prevent the poisoning of the waters. It seems self-evident in the cases of all those rivers from which salmon and sea trout have been exterminated by the poisonous refuse of industrial concerns, that there must be something radically wrong in the administration of the pollution laws. In my humble opinion these are cases for Crown interference, for it is but a farce to leave prosecutions to be undertaken solely by Boards of Conservators whose incomes are very limited and in all cases urgently wanted entirely for preservation purposes.

So turning our backs on these two fishless streams we will make our way to tourist-haunted Machynlleth on the Dovey, a fine river of thirty-five miles in length with a catchment basin of 264 square miles, with the tributaries of the Twymyn fourteen miles, Dulas nine miles, Afon Diflas eight miles, Clwyedog eight miles, and many smaller ones. The Dovey or Afon Dyfi flows from the slopes of Aran Mowddwy in Merionethshire and, after passing through a corner of Montgomeryshire, becomes for a short distance the march between the counties of Cardigan and Merioneth. Dinas Mawddwy is the first village of any importance on its banks, quite a small place, but one with a good large hotel. A few miles below is Mallwyd, then come Cemmes and Machynlleth where the Dulas joins, and some five miles below the Dovey expands into a funnel-shaped estuary about seven miles in length, which at high tide is about the same in breadth. The upper reaches are rocky, with fast-flowing water and plenty of pools and rushes; as it nears the estuary the country becomes so flat and marshy that the gunner-angler will perforce think of the snipe and duck that will, perhaps, assemble there in winter.

In 1860 there were no fixed nets in this estuary or upon the coasts on either sides, but the mouth of the river was fished by public nets using a very small mesh ; a great

3 Z UI

UJ

Q

O

Q

LJ

I

H

part of the tidal water was private, while the first fifteen miles above the tideway was, and still is, in the ownership of Sir William Watkin Wynne, who, with the exception of a few private rights, virtually has the whole of the angling part of the river so far as salmon and sea trout are concerned. The only obstructions at this period were a fishing weir at Mallwyd and a fishing mill dam on the Dulas. The mining industry had not then developed itself, and the Dovey was at this time nearly perfect as a salmon river with its abundance of rapid streams, deep pools and excellent spawning grounds; then by degrees mine pollution began to be the bane of the river, while all expostulations and requests to the mine owners to make settling tanks was met by the cry of expense. Up to about 1850 the Dovey was as good a salmon and sewin river as needs be; then the mining industry came, and as it increased the fish decreased, until there were hardly any left and many fish fresh run with sea lice on them were picked up dead. In 1850 there were plenty of salmon and sea trout in the Twymyn; in 1860 there were none, for the stream ran from week-end to weekend the colour of milk, while so virulent was the pollution that cattle and horses were poisoned to death by eating the herbage that had been covered by the lead water; fortunately the Dovey above the Twymyn junction remained

VOL. I.

unpolluted or otherwise its salmonidce would have been annihilated. Prior to the 1861 Act the close time was for nets and rods from i4th December to 2nd April, though the members of the club that had the whole of Sir Watkin's fishing shifted the opening day to the 2nd May in order to protect the smolts. At this period it was also quite customary for anglers to keep any kelts they caught,

The curtailing of the close time by the 1861 Act was at first a subject of loud and angry complaints freely made by netters and anglers, though both bodies in due course ultimately recognized that the alteration would eventually be to their advantage.

With regard to the pollutions, the late Mr. Ffennell, the then Fishery Inspector, made the following very-much-to-the- point remarks:\Said he, " A miner will go any distance for the water required to work his machinery and clean his ore ; no length of hill or moor will stop him if he can get the necessary fall, and if a land cut will not do he will ingeniously throw wooden aqueducts across the obstructive valleys ; but ask the same men to allow the fish to live in the rivers below them, the poultry to pick up the sand without being killed, the cattle to drink the water or eat the herbage without fear of ' bellan,' and you will find that the expense of digging a few catch pits and of carrying the refuse there bymeans of a ditch, or, may be, of a few fathoms of wooden open pipe, would absorb the whole profits of a mine which, like the Dylifa, employs three hundred hands and raises some two hundred tons of ore a month ! "

In 1867 a Board of Conservators was formed and licences issued for nets and rods, the latter at 205. each. The pollution from the lead mines was still the subject of much complaint.

1869. A very dry season ; no details to be gathered of take of nets or rods.

1872. Some of the lead mines ceased work, when the Twymyn regained its natural colour, and a few salmonidcc ascended; the pollutions from the few mines that still worked had the effect of letting it flow quite clear on each Sunday, when on Monday it once more became a river of milk.

1873 and 1874. 85 salmon rod licences issued at 2os. The netters reported that their takes had been doubled by the cessation of work at some of the mines.

1877. 140 rod licences, some at zos., some at 55. for a month, some at 2s. 6d. for a week, produced .$104. 6s.

1878. in rod licences average 155. each. Close time fixed for nets from i4th September to 3Oth April; for rods, from soth November to ist April. Gaff only to be usedbetween 3ist May and soth October. A free gap was made in the Mallwyd Weir, and the fishing mill dam on the Dulas was not worked.

Chairman of Board: Mr. C. F. Thruston, Talgarth Hall, Machynlleth.

1881. Season rod licences were issued at Iqs., los. month, 55. weekly, 2s. 6d. daily, and produced a total of 125. i2s. 6d.

1882. 66 licences at 20., 74 at icxy., 177 at 5$., 70 at 2s. 6(1. = $156. $s.

1883. Very dry season. 81 licences at 20., 65 at ios., 101 at 5$., 20 at 2s. 6d. Forty convictions for poaching were obtained.

1884. Very dry summer. 78 licences at 2os., 55 at ios., 165 at 5-f., 56 at 2s. 6d. Dry summers do not interfere greatly with the salmon angling, the Dovey being a very late river.

1885. A dry summer, with some disease. 61 licences at 2os., 92 at ios., 155 at 5., 74 at 2s. 6d.

1886. Another very dry season, and one of the worst on record. 80 licences at 2os., 64 at ios., 171 at 55., 51 at 2$. 6d. There was some disease, and thirty convictions for poaching were obtained.

1887. This was a good angling season, though therewas a little disease. The pollutions from the Morgan Gold Mine began to do harm. 87 licences at 2os., no at ios., 174 at 55-., 153 at 2s. 6d.

1888. A good sewin season: an average one for salmon; former attributed to the retaining of the 2-inch mesh net. Still some disease. 109 licences at 20., 111 at ios., 180 at 55., 123 at 2s. 6d. ; a total of 523 anglers.

1889. A poor season for salmon ; fair for sewin. The cost of rod licences was reduced as follows, though there were many people who thought this unwise :\138 season licences at ios. ; 116 monthly at 5. ; 225 weekly at 2s. 6d. ; 434 day at is. ; this produced for 913 anglers a sum of ,$147. i6s. 6d., as against ,$224. 17$. 6d. for 523 anglers in the previous year!

1890. A poor season in all the rivers of the district, except in the Glaslyn; disease was bad, and about 300 fish were buried. The pollution from the gold mine still very serious. 155 licences at ios., 135 at 5$., 221 at zs. 6d., 518 at 15. = ,$164. 15.?. 6d.

1891. A good season on the Dovey, but poor in other streams of the district. A dry summer. It was estimated that the gold mine pollution amounted to 25,000 tons of slime in the season ; no attempts were made by the company to divert it.

1892. A marked increase in the number and weight of salmon in the Dovey, but a decrease of sewin. A number of diseased fish were marked with silver rings in the

*adipose fin and returned to the water in the winter, but none were ever heard of again.
175 licences at ios., 125 at 55., 192 at 2s. 6d., 465 at is. = $166.*

*1893. A dry and bad season, Up till this year the close time for rods had been
between 3oth November and 3Oth April; it was now altered from between 3ist October
to 3Oth April, and no gaff to be used after 3oth September. This alteration led to
considerable friction between the Conservators and the Members of the Club which
had the angling on the fifteen miles of both banks of Sir W. Watkins Wynne's property ;
formed about thirty-five years previously, and long before the Board of Conservators
came into existence, it had been largely instrumental in protecting the Dovey Fisheries
from the effects of mine pollution and poaching. The Club members were limited to
forty, but tickets were issued permitting angling up to the 3151 October to residents and
visitors, while the November angling had hitherto been reserved entirely for the Club
members, and hence the unpopularity of the newly ordained close time. Disease still
lingered. The County Council refused to take any proceedings against the pollutions
of the Gold MineCompany. There were thirty-three convictions for poaching. 145
licences at ios., 144 at 5., 178 at is. 6d., 509 at is. ; 976 anglers = .$156. 45.*

*1894. A dry season, poor for salmon and sewin. The Gold Mine Company promised
to amend their ways. 160 licences at ios., 96 at 5., 170 at 2s. 6d., 328 at is. = $141.
13-y.*

*1895. Again a poor rod season. 121 licences at ios., 115 at 5$., 128 at 2s. 6d., 422
at is. = ,$126. "js. A very heavy reduction from the .$224. 17$. 6d. realized in 1889.*

*1896. A poor season, and very dry for the greater part of it. The Gold Mine
Company did not fulfil their promise, in licences at icw., 103 at 55., 118 at 2s. 6d.,
384 at is.; 716 anglers = 114. 4.*

1897. 83 licences at ios., 107 at 55., no at 2s. 6d., 429 at is. = .$103. 9-r.

*1898. The drought caused another poor season. 104 licences at icw., 89 at 55.,
117 at 25. 6d., 425 at is. 735 anglers = no. 2. 6d.*

*1899. Reported by the Conservators as "below the average." There is one strange
matter in connection with the Fishery Board Reports of the returns made by the
Conservators. The salmon fisheries of each district are ever described as being
"above" or "below" the average, or" much above" the average or " much below"
it, but in no single case is it anywhere stated what the average is computed to be,
an omission which is somewhat puzzling to the student of river lore. Some private
riparian owners brought an action against the Glasdwr Copper Works and obtained an
undertaking that their pollutions should be diverted into settling tanks. 102 licences
at ios., 73 at 55., 75 at 2s. 6d., 265 at is. = $91. 175. 6d.; the lowest amount for
many years.*

*1900. The pollution from the Dylife Lead Mine was taken in hand. The old scale
of rod licence duty was reverted to. 65 licences at 2os., 78 at ios., 91 at 55., 672 at is.
= $160. JS.*

*1901. Good netting, poor rod season. 70 licences at 205., 62 at ios., 58 at 55., 536
at is. = "142. 6s.*

*1902. In this year the old Club was dissolved; it had rented Sir Watkin's angling
for many years practically for nothing, and even then matters financial were only
kept straight by selling an unlimited number of tickets to visitors at Machynlleth and*

Cemmes, and to raise extra funds (for there were but thirty members at the modest sum of .$5 each) they had to net a few days each week in the lower pools, while when the close time was lengthened, the Club closed the river to the public tickets on i5th September,though the members went on angling till the end of October. Thus, when Sir Watkin, seeing the great increase in the value of salmon angling, put a fair rent on the water and offered it to the Club on condition that they did not net and that they placed a limit on the number of rods, this long-existing Association had to break up, as they were unable to raise the amount that was asked for a fresh lease. This was, perhaps, a good thing for the river, which had certainly been much over-fished, as a glance at the number of licences issued will show anyone; of course the innkeepers at Machynlleth and Cemmes, together with the monthly, weekly, and daily fishers, were loud in condemning Sir Watkin's policy, but this feeling will no doubt cool down in due time, and, in my humble opinion, Sir Watkin was absolutely in the right in protecting alike his own interests together with those of the salmon. This fine stretch of water is now let at a considerable rental to Mr. A. W. West, Rhywlas, Machynlleth, who has formed a club of thirty members at ,$25 each, with permission to a few riparian owners at $10 each. Colonel Norton owns a nice stretch of water immediately above Sir Watkin's, a small part on both banks, the remainder on the right one; and here there are six good salmon pools, not counting sewin runs ; throughout the Dovey waders are more or less wanted, not somuch for fishing the pools as for crossing to and fro in order to get a proper command of them ; in low water a 12-ft. rod will do all that is wanted; in high water a i6-ft. rod will be necessary. Colonel Norton sometimes lets his angling when on service with his regiment; there are two good inns handy to it, the " Dovey Valley " Hotel opposite Cemmes Road Station is two miles distant, while the " Penrose Arms," a comfortable, old-fashioned inn in the village of Cemmes, is only half-a-mile from this water, but it cannot put up many visitors; then there are lodgings "of sorts" to be had in the village itself. In Mr. West's water there are fully forty good pools when the river is in order; the Doctors, Twymyn, Cliff, Penybont, Glyndwyr, Cattle Bridge, Sir John's, Ffridd, Bridge Flat, Fir Tree, Dolglennau, and Rhwylas, being some of the chief ones. Salmon begin to run in May, but the best time for prime conditioned fish is from the middle of July (depending on a flood) to the end of August; sewin begin to run in June, and vary from i to 3 Ibs.; salmon average 12 Ibs., and grilse about 6 Ibs. Doctors, Jock Scott, Thunder and Lightning, and other standard patterns will kill; for sewin, large March Browns, claret bodies and gold twist, mallard and claret, and a bumble of blue Andalusian cock's hackle, honey-brown body, gold twist, or peacock herl body with silver twist, which willoften take salmon as well, and can be used all through the district as well as further north and south. Mrs. S. Kemp of Torrington, Devon, ties these flies well. The hour before and the hour after sunset often give the sea trout angler more sport than all the rest of the day, and indeed this is the case throughout the Principality. When the Dulas is in flood, sea trout are often taken in it; there are also a certain number of bull trout, some of them going as heavy as 14 Ibs., but they are seldom caught except as kelts ; the river runs down very quickly after a flood, but then fishes pretty well if worked up stream in low water; trout and sewin are frequently caught in this way, and even salmon occasionally. The Dysynni, " the still river," has its source on the slopes of

Cader Idris, its very head being in the crags above Llyn-y-cae, a deep rocky-shored lake, only some 100 feet below the summit of Idris ; the tiny stream from this high-lying lake goes tumbling down the hillside until it falls into Tall-y-llyn, a beautiful sheet of water a mile-and-a-quarter in length; the outflow from this lake is the Dysynni river, and five miles lower down it passes the slate quarry village of Abergwynolwyn, (the angling down to this point belongs to Colonel Kirkby, of Maes-y-neuadd, and if he is from home, leave is sometimes granted, and in some seasons when he is absent for a long time, tickets are issued for this water).From here it makes a rapid descent to Pont Ystynianer, shortly below which it is joined by the Llanfihangel stream ; from this point the river becomes less rapid, while it is by no means wide, and passing on its tranquil way about four miles nearer the sea it enters the beautiful estate of Mr. R. M. Wynne, of Peniarth, and flowing through his woods and meadows for upwards of six miles, and then beneath the bridge of Tal-y-bont, it shortly forms an estuary. Salmon and sewin rod licences are the same as for the Dovey, and Mr. Wynne kindly permits fishing in his waters at the following rates : season ticket, 4.25. ; monthly, 155. ; weekly, js. 6d. ; daily, 2s. Here, when the water is right, at any time from the beginning of July to the end of September sport with sea trout is nearly certain, for all lures are permitted, while after the i4th September, when the nets come off, there is a very good chance of a salmon.

Some way above Peniarth the river widens considerably, until below the house it becomes a winding, deep lagoon to the sea, into which it opens at Ynys-y-maengwyn ; this lower portion of the river is owned by Mr. John Corbett, and tickets on it may be had at 2os. for the season, js. 6d. a month, 45. a week and is. a day ; with a stiff breeze on it this stretch often gives a good basket of sea trout, and a few heavy salmon after the nets come off; in 1900 these

iX

2 C/l

U X H

took 570 lbs. of salmon; in 1901, 256 lbs. ; in 1902, 300 lbs. Mr. Corbett is loth to use a net, but, as his neighbours above and below use them, he is almost compelled to follow suit; and it is to be regretted that an arrrangement is not come to for abolishing altogether this fresh water netting. Towyn is the best place to stay at, the " Corbett Arms " there being very comfortable. Excepting in times of floods, the waters of the Dysynni are beautifully clear, in the upper reaches the bed being slatey and gravelly and not rocky. At Peniarth Ucha Mr. S. Scott preserves some of the best part of the river. Salmon and sewin ascend to Tall-y-Lynn and spawn in the small streams flowing into the lake, and, though salmon seldom reach it in the open season, a few sewin are caught by the rods in the autumn; its brown trout are famous for the table and doubtlessly have been crossed with sea trout, but as steps have recently been taken to restock the lake with yearling Loch Levens, an improvement in the angling may shortly be looked for.

Small flies are best, and a favourite on the Peniarth Urch waters is the Wickham Fancy. Mr. W. M. Gallichan, in his recently published book, Fishing in Wales, states that in the summer of 1900 an angler had 60 sewin in a week and in September 70 others, a good many being over 2 Ibs. each. The whole stream is only about sixteen miles in

VOL. I.

length, with a drainage of sixty-four square miles. As it flows into the sea by a narrow and shallow channel the fish hang about at the mouth until a flood comes, and during this period of waiting they used to be swept up by the netters, until in 1887 a bye - law was made prohibiting any netting within 300 yards of the mouth of the river.

The Mawddach, or Maw, rises in the wild hills to the north of the Rhobell Fawr (2,313 feet) nearly in the centre of Merionethshire, and after a rapid rush tumbles over the steep falls of Rhiadyr Mawddach, where is situated the Gwynfynydd Gold Mine, that source of obnoxious and wanton pollution : surely if that gold mine is worthy of its auriferous title it should be able to afford the outlay of a little of its gold in making settling tanks, as in doing so it would gain the good-will of the riparian owners, while demonstrating to them and the public that it did not wish to pursue the greedy policy of pouching the uttermost farthing of profit at the expense of the poor fishermen of the estuary and the many others who are concerned in the welfare of the river. The owner of one of the best anglings on the river writes me as follows:\" As to the Mawddach I regret to say it has been ruined for sport by miners and mining operations. The Glasder Copper Mines and the Gwynfynydd, Cefn Dendwr and Afon Coch GoldMines have located themselves on the river, the result being that the pools and spawning beds have been filled up with silt and washings, to say nothing of the attendant pollution caused by the works, and the Mawddach as an angling river is absolutely destroyed."

Shortly below the Falls the river is joined by the Caen, which tumbles over a descent of about 150 feet prior to entering the Mawddach ; two miles nearer the sea the Eden falls in on the right bank and the river continues on its rushing rocky course until Gelligemllyn is reached, where it commences to flow smoothly. Here the Glasder stream enters with the pollutions of the Glasder copper mine ; then flowing under Tyn-y-groes Bridge and by the Inn, it passes on to Llanelltyd to receive the waters of the Wnion at Dolgelly, a short distance below which it enters the Abermaw or Barmouth Estuary, the beauties of which are too well known to need further description here. The total length of the river is about twenty miles, with a drainage area of 151 square miles. The Glasder Copper Mine was started about 1866, and as early as 1869 became the subject of complaint, so much so that the late Mr. Frank Buckland speaks strongly about the matter in his Report to the Fishery Board in 1871.

In 1869 Colonel Romer of Bryncemlin and Mr. Williamsof Dobythel-yuen were very active in protecting the interests of the river : they were at the head of an Angling Association and leasing a net in the tidal water for the three pools below the Bridge ; it was only drawn three days in the week from May to August; in 1869 it took 1,411 Ibs. of salmonida, chiefly sea trout; in 1870 695 Ibs., and in 1871 638 Ibs. Very few were taken in May, 1869 and in 1870 none at all, and in 1871 only n sewin all under 4 Ibs. The poor take of '71 was attributed to heavy floods in July and August which prevented the net from being worked, and the 638 Ibs. that were caught was the result of 26 days' netting. At this period the close time was from 2ist October to March ist, and then for a short time it was altered to November 3oth to April ist, until it eventually settled down to be the same as that of the Dovey. There was also a great deal of poaching, which was very difficult to prevent, for the men hid their spear-heads in the river and cut sticks for handles as they were wanted, their usual plan being to mark fish down in the daytime by means of white stones and then to come and spear them by night. The best angling months are July, August and September, but rainy, stormy weather is almost essential, although in low water the worm cast up stream on fine tackle will account for many fish. During the predominant summer droughts of the nineties the fish

lil

X

H

u.

O

tr

were no doubt subjected to over-netting as they assembled at the mouth to wait for a flood. The river rises and falls rapidly ; wading stockings are necessary; a rod of from 14 to 16 ft. will do the work; small flies are preferable, especially in early summer, and the silver bodies are the favourites, such as Wilkinson, Silver Grey, Silver Doctor and Dusty Miller; Durham Ranger, Jock Scott and Blue Doctor also have their killing days. For sewin, flies with yellow or orange bodies, either mohair or silk, with mallard wing, and very small " Thunder and Lightning," are the most killing, but owing to the silt pollution flies are not so generally used as gold or silver minnows of small size. A small "watchet" bait, which can be bought at Farlow's, is a favourite lure. It is simply a minnow with only one arming; a triangle at the tail.

There are no Angling Associations on the Mawddach, Eden, or Wnion, but Mr. John Vaughan's agent at Nannau issues tickets for that water, which is on both the Mawddach and Wnion, at 42$. for the season, zis. for the month, y. for the week, and 2s. 6d. for the day; these tickets may also be had at Tyn-y-Groes Hotel, while if Captain Bailey, who rents the Hengwrt angling, happens to be away he good-naturedly now and again gives permission to one or two anglers for a day. Salmon and grilse rarely take aworm but come to the fascinations of a silver minnow, a good fish of 14 Ibs. falling to the share of Mr. C. E. Munro Edwards, from the top of Tyn-y-Groes Bridge. One of the best pools on the river is the Llantellydd Pool, just below the bridge on the Hengwrt estate, in which the tide often banks up the water and so may be said to come into it, though perhaps the pool at Tyn-y-groes Bridge is the best of all, but there are others nearly as good in the sections of Gelligemlyn (Mr. H. W. Lee), and the Dolmelynllyn (Mr. C. R. Williams).

Above Tyn-y-groes Bridge Pool, the water is preserved by Mr. R. H. Wood, of Pantglas; Mr. C. E. T. Owen, of Hungwrt-Ucha; and Mr. C. R. Williams. In September, 1900, Mr. Munro Edwards had a day of three fish, of 12, 11, and 6 Ibs., and in all the time he has fished the river and its tributaries, his largest fish has scaled just 17 Ibs. ; salmon average about 10 Ibs., grilse 5 Ibs., and sewin 2 Ibs. The Eden tributary which flows from the Rhinog Fawr (2,362 ft.) has but a course of about fifteen miles, salmon ascending up to the Black Pools, some ten miles above the junction, where Mr. Munro Edwards has caught them ; it formerly fished well in June and July, but owing to the pollution of the main river the angling has much deteriorated ; poaching, too, has had its share in bringing this about ; a grilse rod of 13 or 14 ft. is best here or on the Wnion, as both these streams are more wooded than the main one. The two best beats on the Eden are owned by Mr. R. H. Wood and Mr. J. Nevile West, of Aber Eden, who has about two miles of the left bank, and about a quarter-of-a-mile of the Mawddach, and in one portion both banks of the Eden are also his for a quarter-of-a-mile; the best of the pools here are Dolgefeilian, Old Factory, Llyn Pont ar Eden, and the Junction. The Wnion is a pretty little stream, chiefly kept in the hands of the proprietors, flowing rapidly through a rocky glen by the side of the main road to Dolgelly ; shortly before reaching that town it flows through Mr. Munro Edward's pretty estate of Dolserau Park ; there is no pollution on it, but the river suffers from winter poaching to a certain extent ; salmon and sewin enter it when there is plenty of water, and are later in the season usually accompanied by a few bull trout\Salmo eriox, which the natives call Pisgoddeilen " the trout of the fall of the leaf." A stout trout rod is really all that is necessary, and with one Mr. Edwards has killed grilse up to 6 lbs. ; March Browns and other regular brown trout flies are often effectively used for sewin. To the north of Barmouth, the little river Artro falls into the sea at Llanbedr; it holds a few sea trout, and leave to fish can usually be got by those who stay at the "Victoria" Hotel, though it will be as well to make sure of this before going there.

The Dwyryd, or "the stream of the two fords," runs through the Vale of Festiniog; slate quarries, mines and poachers have pretty well exterminated the fish, and it is harder to catch one sewin now-a-days, where fifty years ago it was an every-day occurrence (with the water in good ply) to catch two or three dozen. The Prysor, which falls into the Dwyryd Estuary is in much the same sorry plight ; neither is it possible to write very much about the Glaslyn, although it does hold a few salmon and sea trout, and from Beddgelert to Portmadoc it is nearly all free fishing or open to the public at very moderate charges.

Close time for nets, from 14th September to 30th April; for rods, from 1st November to 30th April.

Chairman of the Board; Mr. R. O. Jones, Blaenau Festiniog. Clerk: Mr. R. D. Richards, Barmouth.

END OK VOL. I.
,

Lightning Source UK Ltd.
Milton Keynes UK
22 June 2010

155930UK00001B/91/P